Under Benchmarking

in a week

John Macdonald
and Steve Tanner

Headway · Hodder & Stoughton

Acknowledgements

The authors and publishers would like to thank the American Productivity and Quality Center, Houston, Texas and Arthur Andersen and Co. for their help with statistical data and permission to include their Process Classification Framework.

British Library Cataloguing in Publication Data

A catalogue record for this title is available from the British Library

ISBN 0 340 669357

First published 1996
Impression number 10 9 8 7 6 5 4 3 2 1
Year   1999   1998 1997 1996

Typeset by Multiplex Techniques Ltd, St Mary Cray, Kent.
Printed in Great Britain for Hodder & Stoughton Educational, a division of Hodder Headline Plc, 338 Euston Road, London NW1 3BH by Redwood Books, Trowbridge, Wiltshire.

the Institute
of Management
F O U N D A T I O N

The Institute of Management (IM) is at the forefront of management development and best management practice. The Institute embraces all levels of management from students to chief executives. It provides a unique portfolio of services for all managers, enabling them to develop skills and achieve management excellence.

For information on the benefits of membership, please contact:

Department HS
Institute of Management
Cottingham Road
Corby
Northants NN17 1TT
Tel: 01536 204222
Fax: 01536 201651

This series is commissioned by the Institute of Management Foundation.

The authors can be contacted at:

John Macdonald Associates Ltd, 16 Woodcote Avenue, Wallington, Surrey SM6 0QY Tel. & Fax: 0181-647 0160

C O N T E N T S

■ I N T R O D U C T I O N ■

Benchmarking is changing the perspectives of executives and managers around the world. It is showing them how good, bad or mediocre their company is in aspects of their own business as compared with world-class companies. Benchmarking continuously challenges the best practices of modern management. The principles of benchmarking apply equally to manufacturing or service industries, and to large or small organisations.

The growth of benchmarking has been so rapid, and the experience of its use so diverse, that there is confusion as to what the term covers. Some see it merely as an extension to traditional competitive analysis. In truth, however, benchmarking can provide realistic measures and goals for *every* process in the company; and in addition, benchmarking reveals the practices behind company performance.

The aim of this book is to dispel the confusion and provide a step-by-step guide to the understanding of benchmarking and its implementation.

Sunday	–	Understanding the principles
Monday	–	Looking at ourselves
Tuesday	–	Setting the direction
Wednesday	–	Defining how to go about it
Thursday	–	Finding out how others work
Friday	–	Adapting the knowledge
Saturday	–	Staying ahead

What is benchmarking?

Although the concept of benchmarking is quite simple, the full implications and applications of the technique are rarely understood. For example, benchmarking is often mistaken for competitive analysis, or for an excuse for company representatives to visit other organisations – such visits are often related to a current project such as one involving new computer systems. An example of what is *really* meant by benchmarking is that of the coal-mining company that performed a study using Disney World in Florida as a partner. It is difficult to think of two companies with more divergent interests (despite the seven mining dwarfs!). What the coal company was studying was the way in which Disney maintained the pneumatics within their animated characters. Clearly, Disney cannot allow their attractions to loose their lifelike appeal, so they have developed world class maintenance routines for their air-pneumatics systems. The mining company studied these routines and was able to transfer elements back into their own facilities. The resulting decrease in downtime resulted in a major improvement in productivity.

There is nothing new about benchmarking. As Sylvia Codling points out in her book *Best Practice Benchmarking*, benchmarks can be traced back to early Egyptian times when they were used in construction work. A notch was cut in a lump of stone at an accurately determined point whilst a flat strip of iron was placed horizontally to act as the support (or bench) for a levelling staff. Using this as a reference (mark), further heights or distances could then be measured. Today, the term 'benchmark' retains the same meaning in surveying and construction.

The credit for making benchmarking a modern business term is given to the pioneers at Rank Xerox who, in 1979, first started to use the technique in the West. The most famous pioneer, Robert C. Camp, deserves particular mention. It was his first book, *Benchmarking: The Search for Industry Best Practices That Lead to Superior Performance* (1989, ASQC Quality Press, Milwaukee, Wisconsin), which made the Rank Xerox processes and experiences open to all. However, benchmarking was being used in Japan long before 1979. Here, it was being developed in several forms, one of which was the practice of shukko, or the loaning of employees to other organisations. This job-rotation approach encouraged employees not only to learn all about their own organisation's internal business processes, but also to go outside the organisation and bring back new processes to help their organisation move forward. It is from this practice that we take our definition of benchmarking:

> The process of identifying, understanding and
> adapting outstanding practices and processes from
> organisations anywhere in the world in order to help
> your own organisation to improve its performance

You will note that our definition uses the word
'outstanding' rather than 'best': what is 'best' for your
organisation depends on your own unique situation. In
addition, the word 'adapt' has been used rather than
'adopt': benchmarking is not just about observing
outstanding practices and then copying them; for an
outstanding practice to work in your organisation, it is
likely that it will have to be *changed* in order for it to be
made effective.

We must also now give a proper definition for the shorter
term 'benchmark', as this can mean many things. It is:

> A reference or measurement standard for comparison

No mention is made here of 'world-class', 'best in its class'
or any other similar level of achievement. Such
performance levels will be recognised as the standard of
excellence for the particular business process or result, but
the actual level attained will depend on the scope of the
given benchmark. We will therefore be referring to either
'world-class' benchmarks or 'company-class' benchmarks
depending on the scope of the given benchmarking
exercise. But more on this later. First, we must be convinced
that benchmarking will be of benefit to our organisation.

Why benchmark?

A business must change to stay ahead or to get ahead. If a business does not keep up, then its only option is to fall behind competitors. As Deming succinctly put it, 'You do not have to do these things. Survival is not compulsory'. The question now is 'How do we manage the change that is necessary and avoid change that is not necessary?' The act of benchmarking must be carefully managed. Teams get excited about the fun aspects: visiting other companies and learning about their businesses. It is important to channel the energy of this team interest into positive experiences that have a significant payoff for the organisation.

Benchmarking is therefore a managed change process which:

- Uses a disciplined, structured approach
- Identifies what needs to change
- Identifies *how* to change it
- Identifies the potential for improvement
- Creates the desire for change

Benchmarking studies start by focusing on what are the key improvement needs of the organisation. Once the need for change is understood, an examination of best practices and an identification of the key factors that deliver superior performance follow. This in turn will lead to the actions that must be taken. You will also have an idea of the potential for improvement within your organisation, and this in turn will create the *desire* for change as you are now able to visualise the result of the future change as shown in the illustration on the opposite page:

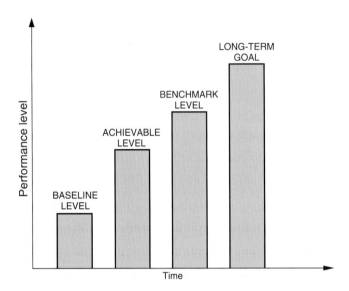

In this figure we see that there are four levels of attainment:

1 the baseline or current performance level
2 the achievable level, which is the best performance that can be achieved using current resources in order to eliminate waste and improve the cycle time
3 the benchmark level, which is the potential level of performance that has been identified from the benchmarking study
4 the long-term goal, which is the future target performance level

The level of your benchmark and the degree of excellence of the process will depend on how far you conducted your search for the best practice. If your search is limited to your own company, then the results of your benchmarking are likely to be limited too. Similarly, if you restrict your search to your own industry alone, then you can only ever become the leader of that industry only. This may well give you a competitive advantage in the short term, but if you want to get ahead and stay ahead, then the name of the game is to return a level of performance that cannot easily be caught. This is where benchmarking scores over other change techniques, such as *business process re-engineering*, which usually rely on internal thinking to deliver superior performance. There are many examples of change implementation where the solutions were unimaginable from within the host industry. The power of benchmarking is that it can encourage thinking 'outside the box'.

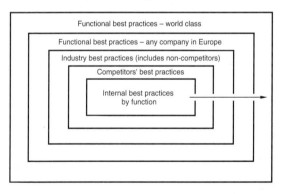

Benchmarking is a step change process. We have already seen from the last diagram that the size of the step is dependent on the scope of the search for the best practice. Benchmarking sits side by side with continuous improvement in that an organisation will always be seeking to improve its performance. Benchmarking will 'kick' the performance of a critical process up to a higher level.

A word about business process re-engineering

As the diagram above indicates, business process re-engineering (BPR) and best practice benchmarking are related. You will discover as we move through the week that one of the first of our activities will be to document and map out the existing processes that are to be benchmarked, and to measure their current level of performance. With BPR there are no strict rules on how the re-engineered processes are derived: it is usually down to the creative talents of the employees of a company. For a more detailed description of BPR, the reader is recommended to read *Understanding Business Process Re-engineering* in this series.

Reasons for benchmarking

Benchmarking helps us to focus on all the business imperatives involved in customer satisfaction, process performance and business results. Any process or practice that can be *defined* can be benchmarked, as for example:

- Strategic planning – practices for developing short- and long-term plans
- Product comparisons – comparing with competitors or best-practice organisations
- Forecasting – predicting trends in relevant areas
- Goal setting – establishing performance goals in relation to state-of-the-art practices

Different types of benchmarking

For the purposes of this book we have divided benchmarking into two main types: *competitive analysis* and *best practice benchmarking*. We will look at both, but we are primarily concerned with the latter.

Competitive analysis
Competitive analysis is often confused with best practice benchmarking. So what is the difference? Well, competitive

analysis will deliver measures against which an organisation can compare its own performance. In this case, however, little is discovered as to how a given level of performance is achieved. For the award frameworks like the Malcolm Baldrige model and the European EFQM Model (see page 57), applicants must show evidence of 'benchmarking'. What an organisation is often performing is competitive analysis to obtain benchmarks against which their own performance can then be compared.

Competitive analysis can be divided into two categories: strategic and tactical. With the strategic focus, organisations are looking for a long-term view to help them with issues such as industry analysis, and with organisational results such as customer satisfaction, employee satisfaction and financial performance. A tactical focus, on the other hand, allows product positioning and measures of process performance. *Reverse engineering* falls into this latter class. This is where a company takes competitors' products, tests them and then strips them down to find out how they have been manufactured. These two categories are illustrated below:

Focus	Market	Business
Strategic	• Industry analysis	• Customer satisfaction
		• Employee satisfaction
		• Community perception
		• Business results
Tactical	• Product positioning	• Process performance
	• Reverse engineering	• Measures

Best practice benchmarking
Best practice benchmarking goes beyond competitive analysis in that here the actual *processes* that deliver the level of performance are uncovered. This is the type of *benchmarking* on which the remainder of this book will focus.

Best practice benchmarking can be divided into four different categories:

- Internal
- Competitive
- Functional
- Generic

Internal best practice benchmarking
This type of benchmarking occurs where a company searches for best practices within its own boundaries. A good example can be found at Kodak, where they have 'Kodak Class' benchmarks defined for all key processes. Through the use of such a system, each location is encouraged to bring its performance up to the level of the internal benchmark, thereby raising the performance of the company as a whole.

Internal benchmarking has the advantage that data is easier to collect because there are fewer barriers to surmount since everybody is in the same boat. The main drawback is that the level of excellence of the results is determined by the level of performance of the best performer *within* the organisation only.

Competitive best practice benchmarking
This type of benchmarking is possibly the most difficult as competitors have a habit of wishing to keep their competitive advantages to themselves. It is more common to have competitors participate in competitive-analysis studies where the espousal of a superior level of performance supports their marketing efforts.

Functional best practice benchmarking
One disadvantage of benchmarking against your competitors is that you will only ever become as good as your best competitor, or will only ever improve on their performance marginally. If your organisation wants to out perform its competitors by a wide margin, then functional benchmarking should be considered. This approach is more difficult since the identification of partners is not as straightforward, but the advantages far outweigh the disadvantages.

The most frequently cited example of functional benchmarking is the case of Rank Xerox and L. L. Bean. Xerox identified L. L. Bean as the industry leader in order-fulfilment and warehousing operations. Xerox then carried out a functional best practice benchmarking study that resulted in the discovery that although Xerox and L. L. Bean had a similar packing process, the L. L. Bean process was three times faster!

Generic best practice benchmarking
One disadvantage of functional benchmarking is that it focuses on the function and not the process. The biggest step changes occur when the function is *not* a barrier to improvement. An example illustrates the point. A team at

DuPont wanted to improve the manufacture of ammunition shells. Customer research had shown that customers wanted 'smoother, shinier shells'. Initially, the team had drawn up a list of traditional internal, competitor and functional partners. They then considered the possibilities outside the industry and settled on a company in the cosmetics industry that made lipstick cases. They found that this manufacturer consistently delivered a product that was smoother and shinier and by coincidence was also shell-shaped! The result of this study was that DuPont was able to improve its processes so that the customers' requirements were fully met.

This is where benchmarking can help. It can be used as a tool to discover alternative practices that can then be implemented so as to deliver superior performance.

Summary

Today we have looked at the background to benchmarking, and have discussed both some misconceptions about the term and the various types of benchmarking available. For the rest of the week we shall concentrate on *best practice benchmarking*. This has the advantage of creating both the performance levels required (the benchmarks) and the *practices* that deliver superior performance. We can close Sunday by summarising the benefits of benchmarking:

- It develops realistic stretch goals and strategic targets
- It establishes realistic action objectives for implementation
- It encourages a striving for excellence, breakthrough thinking and innovation
- It creates a better understanding of competitors and the dynamics of industry
- It emphasises sensitivity to changing customer needs

On Monday we begin by taking a good look at our own organisation and consider where we start the benchmarking journey.

Where do we start?

On Sunday we summarised the benefits that companies
around the world have gained from benchmarking. We are,
therefore, eager to get started but are not quite certain how
or where. A word of caution: benchmarking is not the latest
fad or a quick fix. So before we start, we need to know the
probable level of effort involved and the key elements of
that effort.

The level of effort

Benchmarking is an investment. As a guide to the level of
investment involved, consider the results of a survey that
was commissioned in 1992. This was conducted by the
International Benchmarking Clearinghouse (IBC), part of
the American Productivity and Quality Center (APQC),
which is based in Houston, Texas. The IBC study surveyed
80 leading organisations, and concluded that an average
benchmarking study lasts six months, occupies 25% of team
members' time and costs £45,000. The level of investment
varied depending on the scope of the study, the number of
partners and whether the study was conducted in-house or
with the aid of an outside facilitator.

Clearly, benchmarking represents a substantial level of effort, but aiming to be the best never is – and should never be considered as – an easy task. However, respondents in the above survey indicated that the benefits were nonetheless very significant, with some studies reporting payoffs of more than five times the cost of the study. These returns on investment can take many forms, including:

- Reduced costs
- Increased sales
- Greater customer retention
- Enhanced market share

Over 90% of the respondents indicated that they were going to increase their benchmarking efforts.

The key elements of a benchmarking effort

The elements that an organisation needs to put into place to support an ongoing benchmarking programme are as follows:

- Management support and direction
- A systematic approach
- Research facilities
- Networking
- A code of conduct
- Training for team members and process owners
- An internal database of study plans, programme reports and results
- Internal communication to share successes and learning

The small organisation, however, may not need all these elements on a formal basis.

As we go through today, we shall examine each element in turn.

Management support and direction

Gaining senior management commitment to the benchmarking activities will be crucial to success. If you are a senior executive of your company, then your company is well on the way already: you may just have to convince your colleagues. If you are a manager, then we have already made several key points that will help you construct a convincing argument for benchmarking. It is suggested that you prepare a presentation to your main board in order to gain support.

Once senior management commitment is secured, it is useful to appoint an executive champion. The individual can then form a *steering committee* to oversee the organisation's benchmarking efforts. In this way senior management will play an active role in the benchmarking process.

The role of the benchmarking steering committee can be summarised as follows:

- It guides the selection of benchmarking subjects
- It provides contacts with external organisations
- It promotes benchmarking among senior management
- It supports the benchmarking executive champion
- It integrates benchmarking into different business areas

A systematic approach

Benchmarking should follow a systematic approach to ensure that the process of change is managed effectively. Different practitioners follow different approaches, but they are all fundamentally the same and are based on Deming's Plan–Do–Check–Act cycle. See the following diagram for comparison:

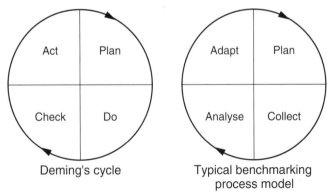

Deming's cycle   Typical benchmarking
                                    process model

Benchmarking process models can be highly detailed, as these examples overleaf show:

The Rank Xerox benchmarking process
Source: Camp,1989

The APQC benchmarking process
Source: APQC The Best of Benchmarking, 1994

Research facilities

If your organisation is new to benchmarking, you will find that there will be new roles and responsibilities. One of these roles is that of the 'research manager' whose prime responsibility is to design, develop and implement information systems, resources and procedures. Research managers provide an on-demand research service to benchmarking teams and maintain an up-to-date benchmarking library. A company would be well advised to recruit a qualified librarian to fill this post. Developing a research facility will include the following actions:

- Monitoring financial, technical and business news about your competitors
- Developing a system to record business measures that makes these measures easily retrievable
- Capturing the measures from internal case histories, such as submissions for the various quality awards
- Creating the organisation and library to continue this service on a long-term basis
- Joining a benchmarking club and getting connected to a benchmarking database

Networking

The ability to find potential benchmarking partners will make or break your benchmarking efforts. Potential partners can be identified in many ways, but there is nothing like knowing an internal contact to open the door to a company and get cooperation.

Most professional benchmarkers have a habit of collecting business cards from everyone they meet. Meeting people at networking meetings and conferences is an ideal way of expanding your network.

Benchmarking clubs
Membership of a benchmarking club is an important element of networking. The typical services offered by a benchmarking club are as follows:

- Member meetings and common-interest groups
- Conferences
- Electronic networking
- A benchmarking database
- Benchmarking facilities
- Research-partner identification
- Training
- Consultancy
- Publications
- Consortium studies

There are European and American benchmarking clubs.
Benchmarking has been practised longer in the USA, so
their level of experience tends to be greater and they have a
wider membership. It is also worth noting that modern
technology has shrunk the Atlantic gap.

Two well-known benchmarking clubs are:

1   The American Productivity and Quality Center
    123 North Post Oak Lane
    Houston
    Texas, USA
    77024-7797
    Tel: (001) 713 681 4020

2   The Best Practice Club IFS
    Wolseley Business Park
    Kempston
    Bedford, UK
    MK42 7PW
    Tel: 44 01234 853605

A code of conduct

'I don't think they play at all fairly,' Alice began, in a rather complaining tone. '... they don't seem to have any rules in particular. At least if there are, nobody attends to them.'

Alice's Adventures in Wonderland, *Lewis Carroll*

Benchmarking relies on international cooperation and professionalism. With organisations exposing their innermost secrets to further the development of others, it is necessary to have some terms of engagement. Adherence to these terms, which are often called a *code of conduct*, contributes to efficient, effective and ethical benchmarking.

Code-of-conduct documents are published by the various benchmarking organisations. These are very detailed documents, but the main principles are listed below:

- Conduct yourself within legal bounds
- Participate by exchanging information
- Respect confidentiality of information
- Use information for the intended purpose only

- Initiate contacts with designated individuals
- Obtain permission before providing contacts
- Be prepared for each benchmarking event
- Follow through with commitments to partners
- Treat information from others as they see fit

Training for team members and process owners

It is suggested that training take place in three phases. The first phase should include both introductory overview presentations for the senior executives and staff-awareness sessions. The second phase comprises the main training course for the benchmarkers, and should include an introductory workshop on benchmarking. This will cover the basics of benchmarking, the benchmarking process to be followed, and other important items like the code of conduct. This workshop will cover significant ground, but it is likely that a specialist tools-and-techniques course will also have to be provided. Finally, the third phase deals with continuing education. Internal workshops have proven useful for keeping benchmarking teams up to date with current practices, and for enabling them to share their experiences. Attendance at external conferences will also provide supplementary education.

Added to these three phases are a host of other training programmes that will support your organisation's benchmarking efforts. These will include programmes on team-based factors and skills such as team dynamics, team leadership and team facilitation.

An internal database of study plans, programme reports and study results

The establishment of an internal database of benchmarking activities will be a useful tool for large organisations, and especially so for those that have many locations or are international. The database can be used to track the progress of benchmarking studies in order to ensure that help is given if any are making slow progress. Once the studies are completed it is important to add the results to the database. This is for a number of reasons:

1 If a search of the database is arranged at the start of a study, it will avoid the embarrassment of duplication. This duplication could occur as a result

either of several teams planning to conduct the same study or of the repetition of a study that has recently been undertaken. It could also be that more than one team is attempting to partner the same organisation, even if it is for different reasons.

2 The database will also serve as both a research source and a way of identifying potential partners.

3 The process of *recalibrating* benchmarks (a topic that we will discuss on Saturday) will be easier to manage as a result.

Internal communication to share successes and learning

Communication has already been mentioned today. It is important that teams share their experiences and that everyone be aware of the results of the studies carried out.

Training and attendance at workshops and conferences have already been mentioned. Several companies produce in-house magazines to promote an awareness of benchmarking, and one should not forget electronic communication as a medium.

One of the most powerful means of communication is to write *targets* into the business plan, which in turn will cascade down to individual or team objectives. The nature of the communication here should be based on benchmarking research into the needs of the organisation.

This whole area is developed in another book in this series entitled *Successful Communication at Work*.

Summary

Today we have considered the preparatory steps for benchmarking. On Tuesday we will get going. However, we do recommend that, in order to gain some preliminary experience, you start your benchmarking activities with a *pilot study*. The steps for a pilot study can be summarised as follows:

1 Present the executive overview and obtain support.
2 Establish and train the pilot team.
3 Select an experienced facilitator to assist the pilot team.
4 Carry out your rigorous benchmarking process.
5 Document the learning gained from the pilot project.
6 Report interim and final results to management.
7 Facilitate the recommended change.
8 Monitor the results of the change.

Starting on Tuesday, and as we move through the week, we shall be examining these steps in detail. Using these steps, our approach will be based on the Plan–Collect–Analyse–Adapt cycle.

The benchmarking roadmap

Today we start our benchmarking journey. To help us on our way, we will follow the benchmarking roadmap as shown in the diagram below:

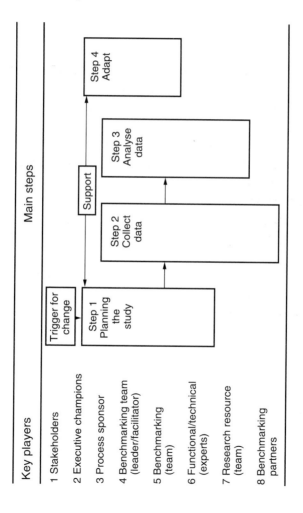

The roadmap on the previous page illustrates the main steps for the pilot study – and indeed for all benchmarking. It also indicates the key players involved. We shall now look at the roles and responsibilities of these players, before going on to discuss the activities involved in each of the main steps.

Roles and responsibilities

It may surprise you that there are so many key players in a benchmarking study. But we shall see that they are all essential as we look at the roles and responsibilities of each in turn.

Stakeholders

Although the stakeholders may not take part in the benchmarking process, they will almost certainly trigger it. The stakeholders could be dissatisfied customers, unhappy shareholders, a regulatory body or even discontented staff. It is the needs of the stakeholders that will be addressed during the benchmarking study, and it does help if the stakeholders can play a part in the study in some way.

In some cases this can be achieved by a representative group of stakeholders working with the benchmarking team or taking part in one of the other roles involved. If, on the other hand, it is not feasible to involve the stakeholders in the benchmaking study, at least their views and expectations can be taken into account when setting the scope of the study. For example, if a world-class performance is required by the stakeholders, then there is little point in restricting your efforts to just an internal benchmarking study.

The stakeholders themselves do not have responsibilities as such since they sit outside the improvement process, but their role does involve a number of relevant elements. These are:

• Creating the need for the benchmarking study
• Helping to set the benchmarking output performance expectations
• Aiding the evaluation of the benchmarking study to see if the objectives were met

The executive champion

The executive champion will typically be the board member who has been given responsibility for overseeing the organisation's benchmarking efforts. This individual will ensure that the benchmarking team is given a clear direction from the board, and that adequate resources are allocated. Senior management will lend its support in other ways, for example by being the advocate of benchmarking, by promoting benchmarking throughout the organisation, and by ensuring that benchmarking teams are recognised for their efforts. This underlines another similarity to business process re-engineering. Without the *singular* drive of the executive champion, progress can drift.

The responsibilities of the executive champion are:

- To ensure that a clear direction is set for benchmarking
- To provide adequate resources for benchmarking studies
- To oversee the implementation of the benchmarking-study recommendations
- To encourage the integration of benchmarking data into strategic planning
- To facilitate the establishment of common performance measurements
- To promote benchmarking activities
- To recognise teams' and individuals' efforts
- To communicate benchmarking to the entire organisation

The process sponsor

Every benchmarking study should have a process sponsor. This individual is someone who is more closely involved in the process to be studied than the executive champion, and who has a direct interest in the output of the study. Process sponsors will be at management level so that they have the necessary influence to make things happen.

The process sponsor has three primary roles. The first is that of *project sponsor*. Here, the responsibilities include providing the resources for a specific benchmarking study and removing obstacles. The second role is that of *process owner*. Here, the responsibilities include management of the process or processes under study and leading the process-improvement effort. Finally there is the role of *process stakeholder*. This is someone who represents other internal processes that have a customer or supplier relationship with the process being studied. The latter also helps with the collection of data.

In a large study it may be that there is more than one process sponsor since here the roles of project sponsor, process owner and process stakeholder are too wide for any one person. This does not affect the benchmarking roadmap in any way since the nature of the involvement of these people remains the same.

We can summarise the responsibilities of the three roles in full as follows:

Project sponsor

- Provides resources, and often initiates the benchmarking study
- Removes initial obstacles to the benchmarking study
- Makes decisions with regard to the project
- Maintains communication and coordinates cross-functional issues
- Assesses the findings of the benchmarking team

Process owner

- Manages the process or processes under study
- Documents the assessment process and approves performance measures
- Identifies problems and opportunities in the current process
- Distinguishes between 'achievable', 'benchmark' and 'long-term' process performance levels
- Leads the process-improvement effort

Process stakeholder

- Represents other internal processes that have either customer or supplier relationships with the process being studied
- Provides an external channel of communication for the organisation
- Serves as a subject expert for the data-collection process

The benchmarking team leader/facilitator

If you are new to benchmarking, then it is advisable to hire the services of an experienced facilitator to keep the benchmarking study on track. If you do have experienced personnel, then it makes sense to make your experienced benchmarking facilitator the team leader as well.

These roles are so important to the success of the benchmarking study that they have been broken down into two. The facilitator is responsible for ensuring that the benchmarking team progresses effectively, and is also there to provide timely training. The team leader on the other hand will manage the project resources, and ensures that all parties are kept informed. The key responsibilities for each role are as follows:

Team facilitator

- Ensures that the benchmarking team proceeds effectively
- Supports the benchmarking team leader
- Provides just-in-time training as the team develops a need for it
- Interfaces with outside resources and ensures that they are used cost-effectively
- Communicates the benchmarking team's progress and results to the rest of the organisation

Team leader

- Manages the project resources on a day-to-day basis
- Negotiates with the process sponsor for appropriate resources
- Ensures that all parties are kept actively involved
- Oversees meetings and the administration of project logistics, and issues periodic reports to all interested parties

The benchmarking team

It is the benchmarking team that will do the bulk of the work during the study. They may also be involved in the identification of the benchmarking-study topic, but for the purposes of this book we will consider only their role during the study itself. This will involve the development and use of benchmarking techniques to collect, analyse and present the relevant data.

Benchmarking team members will be individuals who understand and work with the process being benchmarked. As processes will typically run across functions or departments, the team composition should reflect the key function involved.

The responsibilities of benchmarking team members are as follows:

- Assisting in the development of the study plan
- Designing and producing the data-collection instruments
- Scheduling appointments with data sources
- Gathering data
- Summarising data
- Analysing data
- Identifying performance gaps
- Presenting results
- Producing summary reports

It is worth considering what will make a good benchmarking team member. The seven attributes of a good team member are shown below:

- Process knowledge
- A team player
- Good communication skills
- Good analytical skills
- Innovative
- Time
- A good ambassador

It is not expected that every team member will be skilled in all areas, but a good mix of skills and experience will be essential. Taking each skill in turn:

Process knowledge
Team members must have a solid understanding of the process being benchmarked as well as being well versed in the benchmarking process itself. One of the most frequent complaints on the part of sought-after benchmarking partners is that *unprepared* benchmarkers are corrupting

the process. This is why one of the first steps in formulating a benchmarking team is to provide benchmarking training, so that there is a common understanding.

A team player
The benchmarking team will be working together for an extended period of time. There may be personality clashes during this time, but as long as all the team members are good team players this should not be a problem. The attributes of good team players are that they listen to others, are committed to the team's success and not just their own success, support each other and all make a contribution.

Good communication skills
Communication will be one key factor in the success of the project. This will involve both verbal and written as well as visual communication. For example, there will be people to talk to, reports to write and presentations to be made. Team members will have to communicate with a range of people from customers and suppliers to process operators, to benchmarking partners and to senior management, to name but a few.

Good analytical skills
Team members should feel comfortable dealing with data. They must be numerate and have a grasp of basic mathematical techniques.

Innovative
Good benchmarking team members are willing to seek out new ideas, discover what is behind superior practices and break through existing paradigms.

Time
Most benchmarking studies last around three to six months, and as a rule of thumb, team members will spend approximately 10 hours per week on a study.

A good ambassador
When site visits to partners take place, the benchmarking team members involved become ambassadors for their organisation. Senior management must feel confident that all team members will leave the partners with a favourable impression of their organisation.

Functional/technical experts

In many industries there will be a need to consult experts. For example, in the life-insurance industry, where the provision of service is surrounded by legislation, it would be unthinkable to tamper with existing processes without a consideration of the legal implications.

Functional and technical experts can also be useful in other ways, for example in identifying possible benchmarking partners and defining functional characteristics when attempting generic benchmarking studies. They are also of value during the analysis of data, and particularly when the data has to be normalised.

The responsibilities of the functional/technical experts are:

- The provision of technical advice
- Help with the identification of potential benchmarking partners
- Assistance in defining key attributes for global benchmarking studies
- Aiding the collection and analysis of data

The research resource team

The need to establish a research resource team was discussed on Monday. The main responsibilities of the research resource team are:

- Designing, developing and implementing information systems, resources and procedures
- Providing an on-demand research service to the benchmarking team using external databases
- Identifying and acquiring new information sources for the benchmarking technical library
- Maintaining a file of all benchmarking non-disclosure agreements
- Managing the use of external suppliers of information services

Benchmarking partners

Where it is expected that your organisation will conduct
benchmarking in an ethical and professional manner, it is in
your company's interest for your benchmarking partners to
behave in a similar fashion. Benchmarking is all about the
mutual exchange of information that benefits all parties,
and it will not be in your interest if one of your partners
passes your industry secrets to your competitors. It is
therefore recommended that you encourage your partners
to agree to conform to a code of conduct. This is indeed the
main responsibility of a benchmarking partner. If your
partners are experienced benchmarkers, this will not be a
problem. If, however, one of your partners is not
experienced and will not agree to conform to a code of
conduct, it may be in your interests to reconsider the
organisation as a potential partner.

Summary

Today we have outlined the benchmarking roadmap. To
complete today's study we shall now briefly list the tasks
ocurring in each step of this roadmap in preparation for
Wednesday, Thursday and Friday, when we shall be getting
to the thrust of the study.

The individual tasks in each benchmarking step that we
have considered today are as follows:

Step 1: Planning The Study

- Form a benchmarking team
- Establish the process to be benchmarked

- Document the current process
- Define the topic areas for data collection

Step 2: Collecting Data

- Identify potential benchmarking partners
- Plan data-collection methods
- Conduct a primary investigation
- Prepare for site visits
- Conduct site visits
- Write site-visit reports

Step 3: Analysing Data

- Normalise performance data
- Construct a comparison matrix
- Identify best practices
- Isolate process enablers

Step 4: Adapting

- Communicate findings and gain a commitment to change
- Set goals to close the gaps
- Adapt enablers
- Develop an implementation plan and implement it
- Monitor and report progress

We have now considered the tasks and the roles and responsibilities of those involved in benchmarking. Tomorrow we move onto the first stage: planning the study. As part of that phase we shall need to select a process to benchmark, and to help us we shall be looking in detail at the Process Classification Framework. By way of an introduction, the *main* operating, management and support processes of this framework are illustrated opposite.

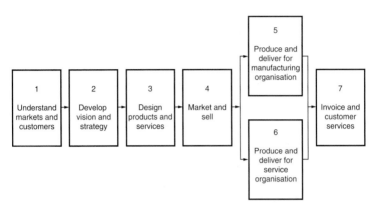

Process Classification Framework: operating processes

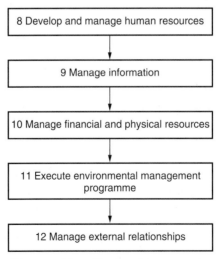

Process Classification Framework:
management and support processes

Planning the study

Today we move on to the first main step outlined on the benchmarking roadmap illustrated on page 31: 'Planning the study'. The tasks involved in planning the study are as follows:

- Form the benchmarking team
- Establish the process to be benchmarked
- Document the current process
- Define the topic areas for data collection

Forming the benchmarking team

On Tuesday we covered the roles and responsibilities of the benchmarking team, so there is not much more to add here. It is useful, however, for the benchmarking team to create a *team charter* which will help guide them through the coming months. The team should also start to document the activities that will be taking place as the study gains momentum, and to draft a study plan. The study plan will contain the outputs of the tasks that we shall be going through today.

Establishing the process to be benchmarked

The most important question that can be asked when selecting the subject for a benchmarking study is 'What factors will have the greatest impact on the performance of the organisation?' Because benchmarking is often a lengthy and expensive process to support, an organisation should only engage in the process when the latter appears capable of adding value to the bottom-line results of the business. Benchmarking is not the process of choice involved when investigating routine matters or issues of low to moderate importance. Nor is it to be advocated when it is solely to be used as an information-gathering technique.

At the commencement of a benchmarking study an organisation should identify several 'critical success factors' or CSFs. It is from these CSFs that the process for benchmarking will be chosen. The identification of the CSFs and the link to the business's success is a process in itself. In benchmarking studies, the call for action is sometimes unambiguous: in certain cases a manager commissions a specific project, and in other situations an individual or team identifies a specific problem or opportunity for benchmarking on the basis of some obvious need. In these situations the identification of CSFs may be straightforward. However, there will be times when an individual or team will only be provided with a general direction, with no clear indication of the *particular subject* of the benchmarking effort.

Today we are going to look at an approach that will help you both to define your process for benchmarking and to ensure that the chosen subject is not only aligned with the direction of the business but will also support an improvement in the bottom line. This approach will use the Process Classification Framework we introduced on Tuesday.

We shall also be looking at another way of arriving at your subject for benchmarking: by evaluating the output from an assessment against one of the total-quality frameworks. For this we shall be considering the UK and European quality models illustrated later today.

Where is the company going?
Most companies have a vision statement or mission statement, or even both, and now we are adding critical success factors (CSFs). It is very easy to become hooked up on terminology, and so it is useful here to define what we mean by these terms.

- Vision: a statement that describes the desired future position of the company. For example, 'We will become a world-class provider of consultancy services'
- Mission: a statement that describes the purpose of the organisation. For example, 'We provide cost-effective consultancy services that delight our clients and cause measurable improvements in their business'
- Critical Success Factor: a statement describing a characteristic of the business which, if not delivered, would cause the non-achievement of either the vision or the

> mission. For example, a business
> becomes complacent and as a result
> ceases to be a 'world-class' or 'cost-
> effective' consultancy

The development of vision and mission statements has
been described in another book in this series entitled
Understanding Total Quality Management.

Critical success factors can be developed from the
organisation's vision and mission statements. The best way
to do this is to use a technique called *brainstorming*. Here,
the executive management team or the steering committee
considers the vision and mission statements in turn and
records every individual's suggestion for a potential CSF.
Ideally, a CSF should consist of two words, one a noun and
the other an adjective. When brainstormed in this manner,
the results are clear and simple to handle. At the end of the
brainstorming session, the executive team should select –
and even combine – the various suggestions to provide a
maximum of five CSF statements. These should be simple
and easy to understand, and everyone should accept them.

This kind of session is also a powerful exercise in gaining
executive involvement and commitment.

Identifying the critical processes
The identification of an organisation's critical processes is a
complex task. It usually includes considering a host of data
on factors including customer satisfaction, employee
satisfaction, the vision and mission, process performance
and business results. A quick way of deciding which

process should be put forward for benchmarking is by using the Process Classification Framework introduced on Tuesday. This is a high-level, generic enterprise model that can be used in any organisation. Its purpose is to facilitate cross-industry benchmarking by defining an organisation's activities from a process and not a functional viewpoint. The Framework has seven 'operating processes' and six 'management and support' processes. These are the high-level processes, and under each high-level process there are a number of sub-processes. By using the Process Classification Framework as a checklist, you will be able to make a list of those critical processes that underpin the delivery of your CSFs. You will need these for the next section of our work. The detailed Process Classification Framework is illustrated in the following diagram. There is even a lower level that goes into the detail of *individual* tasks. It might help you to get a copy of the complete process listing for inclusion in your reference library. Copies are available from the American Productivity and Quality Center, whose address was given on page 25.

1 Understand markets and customers

1.1 Determine customer needs and wants
1.2 Measure customer satisfaction
1.3 Monitor changes in the market or customer expectations

2 Develop vision and strategy

2.1 Monitor the external environment
2.2 Define the business concept and organisational strategy
2.3 Design the organisational structure and relationship between organisational units
2.4 Develop and set organisational goals

3 Design products and services

3.1 Develop new product/service concepts and plans
3.2 Design, build and evaluate prototype products and services
3.3 Refine existing products/services
3.4 Test the effectiveness of new or revised products/services
3.5 Prepare for production
3.6 Manage the product/service-development process

4 Market and sell

4.1 Market products/services to relevant customer segments
4.2 Process customer orders

5 Produce and deliver for manufacturing-orientated organisation

5.1 Plan for and acquire necessary resources
5.2 Convert the resources or inputs into products
5.3 Deliver the products
5.4 Manage the production and delivery process

6 Produce and deliver for service-orientated organisation

6.1 Plan for and acquire necessary resources
6.2 Develop human-resource skills
6.3 Deliver the service to customers
6.4 Ensure quality of service

7 Invoice and service customers

7.1 Bill the customer
7.2 Provide after-sales service
7.3 Respond to customers' enquiries

Operating processes

8 Develop and manage human resources

8.1 Create and manage human-resource strategies
8.2 Cascade strategies down to the work level
8.3 Manage the deployment of personnel
8.4 Develop and train employees
8.5 Manage employee performance, reward and recognition
8.6 Ensure employee well-being and satisfaction
8.7 Ensure employee involvement
8.8 Manage labour-management relationships
8.9 Develop human-resource information systems

9 Manage information resources

9.1 Plan information-resource management
9.2 Develop and deploy enterprise-support systems
9.3 Implement systems security and controls
9.4 Manage information storage and retrieval
9.5 Manage facilities and network operations
9.6 Manage information services
9.7 Facilitate information sharing and communication
9.8 Evaluate and audit information quality

10 Manage financial and physical resources

10.1 Manage financial resources
10.2 Process finance and accounting transactions
10.3 Report information
10.4 Conduct internal audits
10.5 Manage the tax function
10.6 Manage physical resources

Process Classification Framework:
management and support processes

11 Execute environmental management programme

11.1 Formulate an environmental management strategy
11.2 Ensure compliance with regulations
11.3 Train and educate employees
11.4 Implement a pollution-prevention programme
11.5 Manage remediation efforts
11.6 Implement emergency-reponse programmes
11.7 Manage government-agency and public relations
11.8 Manage acquisition/divestiture environmental issues
11.9 Develop and manage environmental issues
11.10 Monitor the environmental management programme

12 Manage external relationships

12.1 Communicate with shareholders
12.2 Manage government relationships
12.3 Build lender relationships
12.4 Develop public-relations programmes
12.5 Interface with the board of directors
12.6 Develop community relations
12.7 Manage legal and ethical issues

13 Manage improvement and change

13.1 Measure organisational performance
13.2 Conduct quality assessments
13.3 Benchmark performance
13.4 Improve processes and systems
13.5 Implement total quality management (TQM)

Which process to benchmark?

To determine which process to benchmark, your benchmarking team now has the task of correlating the CSFs with the critical processes that have been identified. To do this, complete the following steps:

1 Draw up a matrix, with the CSFs down the left-hand column and the critical processes along the top.

2 Working down each process column, rate the importance of each process for each CSF using the following scale:

   1 = low impact
   3 = medium impact
   5 = major impact

   Write the impact rating in the top (left) half of each box.

3 Now rate the performance of each critical process using the following scale:

   1 = excellent performance
   3 = average performance
   5 = poor performance

   Write the process performance rating in the horizontal column provided at the top.

4 Multiply the CSF impact rating by the process performance rating for each critical process to get the *improvement priority score.* Enter the result in the bottom (right) half of each box.

5 Total the priority scores for each process. The result will
   give a measure of the degree of importance, in terms of
   improvement, of each of the critical processes. The
   highest-scoring process is the one that should be
   selected as the prime candidate for the benchmarking
   study.

The calculation described above is shown graphically in the
diagram below. This exercise has assumed that there are
five CSFs and three critical processes.

Rating for impact of critical
process 1 on CSF 1

	Critical process 1	Critical process 2	Critical process 3
Process performance rating	3	5	1
CSF 1	3 / 9	1 / 5	3 / 3
CSF 2	5 / 15	1 / 5	3 / 3
CSF 3	3 / 9	5 / 25	5 / 5
CSF 4	3 / 9	3 / 15	3 / 3
CSF 5	5 / 15	1 / 5	5 / 5
Total priority	57	55	19

Improvement priority score for critical process 1

Highest priority for benchmarking

Second highest priority for benchmarking

Lowest priority for benchmarking

The EFQM Model

There is another important way to assess the key processes or practices to be benchmarked. This is by using the European Foundation for Quality Management's Total Quality Model (the EFQM Model). The EFQM Model is widely used in the United Kingdom and other major countries of the European Union.

The basic principles of the EFQM Model are illustrated in the diagram on the opposite page. Leadership drives policy and strategy, human and other resources through a series of processes. These processes serve both to increase customer satisfaction and people satisfaction and to make an impact on society, and this in turn ultimately produces business results.

The EFQM Model is used to assess an organisation against certain criteria. Qualified assessors will evaluate a company and its practices and produce an Assessment Score which is in fact benchmarking the organisation against the varying criteria. The diagram shows five sets of criteria known as *enablers,* followed by four criteria that address the *results* obtained as a consequence of the *use* of these enablers. In the assessment process, a maximum of 1,000 points are available. These points are divided equally between the enablers and the results.

There is a growing wealth of evidence to show that organisations that score well against the EFQM Model deliver outstanding business results. It therefore follows that using the Model's criteria as an initial benchmark will lead to an improved business performance.

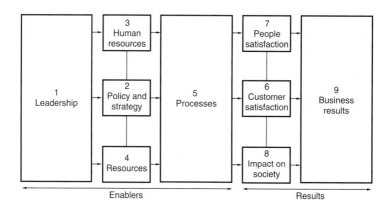

Using the results of an assessment

We do not have the time to discuss in detail the process of conducting an assessment, but we *can* provide a summary as follows.

The easiest way to undergo an assessment is to enter a submission for either the European Quality Award or the UK Award, both of which are based on the EFQM Model. You will have to complete a self-assessment document, in which you will describe your organisation's approach in the enabler areas covered by the Model: leadership, policy and strategy, human resources, resources and processes. The judges will be considering both the degree of excellence of your approach and the degree of deployment in these areas.

For the results sections, you will report your current level of performance against your own targets and, if known, the best competitors' performance. Results are required for: customer satisfaction, people satisfaction, impact on society (or the community's perception of your company and your efforts to preserve the environment) and business results. The judges will be considering both the degree of excellence, in the areas of the model that you report results for, and the *scope* of your results, in terms of the areas of the business that are covered.

Your reward for entering for an award will be a detailed feedback report. In this report the judges will give you feedback on every part of the model, together with an idea of your score against each particular section. Against each area, they will list the strengths you have together with their view of areas for improvement.

From the scores and feedback comments provided, it will be easy to establish a shortlist of candidate processes for benchmarking. What's more, the assessment of your organisation against the various areas of the Model will be aided by the fact that there is a vast amount of information describing the approaches and results of the various previous award winners.

Documenting and mapping the current process

Now that we have chosen the particular process for benchmarking, we need to define and document the current process. Process diagrams and process maps are used for this activity. The design and completion of process diagrams and maps are fully described in companion books in this series entitled *Understanding Total Quality Management* and *Understanding Business Process Re-engineering*.

The steps that are needed for a process-mapping activity are illustrated in the diagram below, and can be defined as follows:

- Identify the customers of the process
- Determine the customer requirements for the process outputs
- Determine the measures
- Analyse the activities that produce the process outputs
- Determine the input requirements
- Identify the suppliers to the process

Identifying the customers of the process
Develop a thorough understanding of the customers of the process, and analyse them by market segment, demographics, trends etc. where appropriate. Phone interviews, surveys and focus groups are good ways of obtaining customer feedback.

Determining the customer requirements for the process outputs
These are your customers' measures of success. These measures provide the basis for determining how well you are meeting customer expectations. The requirements will typically be grouped into two categories: 'hard' measures and 'soft' measures.

Determining the measures
The hard measures are those to which you can attach definite performance data. Examples are:

- Cost (labour costs, material costs, product/service costs)
- Quality (error rates, complaint levels, defect levels)
- Cycle times (production time, delivery time, response time)

The soft measures are the measures of perception. Examples are:

- Customer satisfaction
- Employee satisfaction
- Community satisfaction

It is important to identify measures that will provide a meaningful basis for comparing your process with those of other organisations.

Analysing the activities that produce the process outputs
This means defining the beginning and ending points, and
understanding every activity in between: who performs
them, how long they take, and so on. A flow chart provides
a visual tool for communicating with key process players.

Determining the input requirements
List all the products or services, or both, that you need to
produce the output. Identify the measures of success for
each.

Identifying the suppliers to the process
A similar desire for process improvement is also required
on the part of your *suppliers* who are often sources of
valuable information about industry trends and best-in-the-
class performance.

Defining the topic areas for data collection

Now that the initial analysis has been completed, it is just a
matter of defining exactly which parts of the process – or it
may be the entire process – are to be benchmarked. It is
also possible that your investigation has identified areas of
performance that, up to now, you have not even measured.
To complete the planning stage you should record what
processes are to be studied, what the process measures are,
and the current levels of performance. If possible, record
the results over an extended period to see what the current
rate of improvement is.

Summary

Today we have looked at the planning stage of the benchmarking study. We have considered two methods for identifying potential processes for benchmarking. The Process Classification Framework method, involving the vision and mission statements and the critical sucess factors (CSFs), will allow you to benchmark those processes that will have a maximum impact on your organisation's success. The second method based on the EFQM Model, will also have a positive impact on the business, and will put your organisation within a recognised total-quality framework.

Now that we have identified what process we are going to benchmark and have planned the study, tomorrow we can look forward to collecting the data.

Collecting the data

Today we move on to the second main step outlined on the benchmarking roadmap, shown on page 31: 'collect data'. The main tasks involved in collecting the data are:

- Identify potential benchmarking partners
- Plan the data-collection methods
- Conduct a primary investigation
- Prepare for a site visit
- Conduct the site visits
- Write the site-visit report

The collection-of-data stage is a graduated discovery process that has four main phases:

1 internal analysis
2 external research
3 a primary investigation
4 a site visit

The first phase, internal analysis, concerns the collection of data about the process to be benchmarked. This was conducted under the 'Planning the study' phase, and it ended with a definition of the process or processes to be benchmarked, the performance measures and the current level of performance.

The next phase is to conduct external research in order for potential partners to be identified. This is followed by a primary investigation where potential partners are contacted and screened for suitability: there is no point in conducting a site visit to a customer if the performance level of the possible partner is below the current performance level of your own organisation.

The final phase is where a site visit is conducted to get the details on the best practices of the partner. Although the prospect of a site visit is attractive, they tend to be time-consuming and expensive. As a result, the number of site visits in a study is limited to between four and six. Some organisations choose not to go through the site-visit stage but instead to finish their study at the primary-investigation stage. For the purposes of this book, however, we shall assume that the study will follow the full process.

- Internal analysis
  - • Map current process
  - • Define measures
  - • Record current performance levels

- External research
  - • Search for potential partners

- Primary investigation
  - • Collect initial data from potential partners
  - • Shortlist partners for site visit

- Site visit
  - • Visit shortlisted partners
  - • Discover best practices
  - • Document findings

Identifying potential benchmarking partners

On Monday we discussed the need to set up a research facility within your organisation. This facility will mainly be used in the identification of potential partners. A literature search should be conducted of all the articles, reports, conference papers etc. that are in your library to see if any potential partners can be found. It is surprising how much data is available in the public domain that can be obtained by reading documents such as company reports and trade articles. Robert Helms, a former CIA agent, is credited with saying that over 85% of all CIA research comes from an appropriate analysis of open literature. This is why a well-kept, up-to-date and indexed library will be a valuable time saver.

Another invaluable source of information comes from searching the database of one of the benchmarking clubs. This is where American benchmarking clubs score over the European ones since their databases are more extensive.

One question to consider is 'How recent and reliable is the information?' It is also important to be confident that the information uncovered is sufficient to give a reliable indication of a potential partner's performance.

At the end of this stage you should have a list of potential partners. Now you must screen these partners so you can decide which ones should be approached for a site visit.

The following diagram puts this section into perspective and gives some useful additional sources of external research data. It has been adapted from material published in Michael Porter's *Competitive Strategy*.

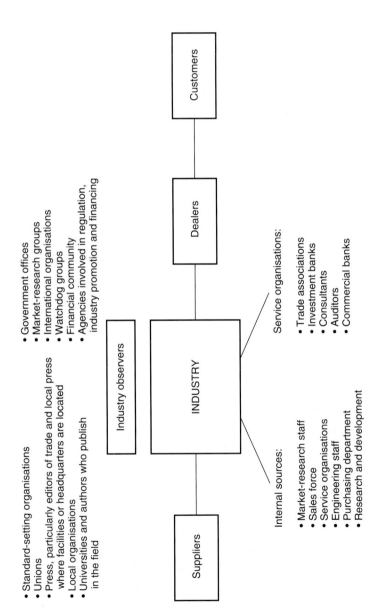

Industry observers
- Standard-setting organisations
- Unions
- Press, particularly editors of trade and local press where facilities or headquarters are located
- Local organisations
- Universities and authors who publish in the field
- Government offices
- Market-research groups
- International organisations
- Watchdog groups
- Financial community
- Agencies involved in regulation, industry promotion and financing

INDUSTRY

Suppliers — Dealers — Customers

Internal sources:
- Market-research staff
- Sales force
- Service organisations
- Engineering staff
- Purchasing department
- Research and development

Service organisations:
- Trade associations
- Investment banks
- Consultants
- Auditors
- Commercial banks

Planning the data-collection methods

For data collection to be effective, you need to do it in a structured way. The best way is through the use of a *questionnaire*. These do not have to be sent through the post, although this *is* the most usual method. Two other methods to consider are the telephone interview and the face-to-face interview – we shall be dealing with the face-to-face interview during our discussion on site visits. The telephone interview has the advantage over a postal questionnaire in that it is more interactive, and there is also less of a perceived effort on the part of the interviewee. A disadvantage, however, is that at the particular time when the telephone contact is made, the interviewee may not have all the data you require to hand.

Questionnaire development is quite a complex task, which all too often is taken too lightly with disastrous results. Let's consider the design of a generic questionnaire that will help you to design your own *specific* questionnaire. The steps we shall follow are noted below:

- Produce a draft questionnaire
- Pilot the draft questionnaire internally
- Pilot analysis of the completed draft questionnaires
- Agree to the final questionnaire
- Carry out a second pilot study if necessary

Produce a draft questionnaire
The first step in designing a questionnaire is to get an agreed objective for the questionnaire. Then, once you have completed the design of the questionnaire, you can test it against the achievement of this objective. An example of a draft benchmarking questionnaire is illustrated overleaf.

1 How do you define the successful process of yours that is under study? Please describe it.

2 What is the measure of quality for this process? What are the criteria you use to define excellence in the process performance? How do you measure the output quality of this process? How do you measure progress in quality improvement?

3 What is the current performance level of this process? Please give quantitative results and indicate the past performance six months ago and 12 months ago if available.

4 How do you evaluate the cost and timeliness of this process?

5 Do you consider the process to be in control? How do you know?

6 Do you consider this process to be a problem or concern to your company? If not today, was it a problem in the past?

7 How much and what type of training do you provide for the various job categories of the process team?

8 What process improvements have given you the best return in performance improvements?

9 What company, excluding your own, do you believe is the best in performing this process?

10 Do you have any other information that you think will help us?

The questions presented in this example fall into six major categories:

- Process definition
- Process measurement
- Process performance
- Process problems
- Process improvements
- Process enablers

The first question is an open question designed to get your potential partners describing something they enjoy: their successful process. All the other questions are broad open questions, except for the performance-level questions. At this questionnaire stage you are trying to get an idea about the level of excellence of the process so that you can narrow the field for site visits. Detailed questions probing exactly how the best practice performance is achieved will be used during the site visit.

If you do not intend to follow up with site visits, it is important that you include some more specific questions that seek to uncover the *enablers* (see page 50) behind the best practices. For example, you may ask respondents to include a map of the process, a copy of the current process procedures or a copy of the latest performance figures.

Pilot the draft questionnaire internally
It is well worthwhile piloting the survey internally before sending it to your potential partners. This is for two reasons. First, the questions must be easy to understand, not ambiguous. If a pilot group goes through the questionnaire first, any problems of this nature will be eliminated. It is also useful if you can include someone outside your immediate area in your pilot group, perhaps a supplier or a customer: quite often the questionnaire can be full of company jargon and three-letter acronyms, and although it may make sense to you, to an outsider it might look like a foreign language! A second reason for piloting the questionnaire internally is that it will add to the data you already have on the process in your own organisation. This will complement your internal analysis.

A final check on the questionnaire is to make sure that every question makes a valuable contribution to achieving the objective of the study. One of the biggest turn-offs for a potential partner is when they are faced with a host of questions that they think are going to take a lifetime to answer. Any action to simplify or shorten the questionnaire will therefore be warmly welcomed by the potential partner.

Pilot analysis of the completed draft questionnaire
There is nothing worse than expending enormous effort on a survey only to find that you cannot make head nor tail of the answers! It is therefore crucial that the results of the pilot questionnaire are analysed to ensure that the exercise will give you the answers that you are seeking.

Once the analysis is complete you should check the result against the objective you set at the start. If the objective is met that's good. If not, it is time to rethink the questionnaire.

Agree to the final questionnaire

The benchmarking team should get a sign-off once they are confident that the analysis will lead to meeting the objectives of the study. The questions should also be easy to understand and add value in achieving the final goal.

It is better if the questionnaires are professionally printed before they are sent to the potential partners. When the potential partners look at the questionnaire they will get an impression of your company and a questionnaire on lightweight paper produced on a photocopying machine that leaves marks on the paper, or is misaligned, will not project a good image. If the questionnaire is printed then the potential partner will consider that you are taking the exercise seriously.

Carry out a second pilot study if necessary

If the trial produced many changes or amendments to your original questionnaire, it may be worthwhile conducting a second pilot. This may slow down your benchmarking study but the delay will ensure that your study will be successful.

Conducting a primary investigation

Now that the questionnaire is designed we can move onto the primary investigation. When sending your questionnaire to your potential partners the questionnaire should be accompanied by a letter from a high-ranking official which describes the reason for the approach. The letter should do the following:

- State who is writing and their position
- Define the study topic and objectives
- Extend the invitation to participate in the study
- Commit to send all participants a copy of the summary report at the end of the study
- State who you would like to complete the questionnaire
- State when you would like the questionnaire returned by (you should allow about four weeks from the date of the letter)
- Reinforce that your company abides by a code of conduct and that the results will only be used for internal purposes
- Provide a contact point that will be available to answer questions and issue additional copies of the questionnaire
- Include *your* telephone number so that participants can contact *you*

It is a good idea to send a copy of the questionnaire completed for your organisation with the invitation. This shows that you are prepared to be open in the sharing of information and it can be used as an example of the responses you are looking for from the potential partner.

Once all the questionnaires have been returned, or when the return date has passed, the questionnaires should be analysed. If any of the data in the questionnaires is incomplete then you should telephone the respondent to fill in the missing gaps. It is now time to shortlist the potential partners for site visits. This involves comparing and ranking them in various categories.

Preparing for a site visit

Visiting other organisations is usually the most useful means of collecting detailed data on companies. They are particularly well suited for identifying process enablers, which are the methods, documents, training or techniques that facilitate the successful implementation of the benchmarked process. Other objectives include:

- Gaining an insight for the interpretation of metrics
- Observing work processes
- Improving the understanding of process information
- Understanding the impact of the culture on the process
- Developing long-term relationships for effective sharing

It has already been mentioned that site visits are expensive and so it is imperative that as much as possible is gained from the visit. This is achieved by careful planning.

We advocate a two-step process for the site visit. First a 'metrics and practices' questionnaire should be sent to the partner requesting detailed process performance data. From the analysis of this questionnaire and the knowledge of your own process, a second questionnaire should be developed that focuses on the gaps in performance. This second questionnaire should be limited to just the core issues and be no more than 20 questions. It should be sent to the partner at least four weeks before the visit.

Before the site visit you should get your partner's agreement to an agenda. A good way of starting the site visit is to get the partner to give a presentation that addresses the questions set. There should also be agreement to the code of conduct that will be followed by both parties.

The benchmarking team must also prepare for the site visit. It is a good idea to produce a 'site visit kit' and hold a pre-visit briefing which addresses:

- The meeting agenda
- The questions set
- Organisation information (primary investigation findings, secondary research information, metrics and practices questionnaire results, annual report, key contacts, etc.).
- Meeting and travel arrangements

One final point that should be considered is that it is wise to leave your 'best' partner until last. This will allow a period of learning for the benchmarking team before this partner is visited.

Conducting the site visits

All team members should attend the site visit, and the proceedings should be tape-recorded with permission from your partner. Be flexible about sticking to your agenda: some, perhaps more experienced, partners will want to take the lead, and it is important not to digress but to focus on the critical issues. Above all, make sure that you record:

- Best practices
- Process enablers
- Topics for future information sharing
- Commitments to follow up with additional information

During the discussions, remember to 'give as good as you get': the interviews are an exchange of information and not just a one-way process. Always observe the code of conduct, and respect sensitive topics. Finally, decide the next steps before you leave. This will strengthen the long-term relationship with your partner.

After the site visit, follow up on any documents or information that you requested, or that you agreed to supply.

Writing the site-visit report

The site-visit tape should be transcribed as soon as possible after the site visit. The team should review what they 'heard' during the site visit and document best practices right away to aid analysis. Agreement should also be reached on the process enablers.

The site-visit reports should be brief and follow a consistent format. They should include:

- A company overview
- A report on best practices identified
- A report on enablers to be used

It is courteous to send a copy of the final site-visit report to the partner. It may be that there is something that you have misinterpreted, or that they can add value to the report in some other way.

When all the site visits have been completed, you should conduct a process and an enabler analysis. In the process analysis you should code and organise practices by category. Incorporate key metrics, together with a narrative to highlight performance gaps. Remember that there may be some best practices in your own organisation that you should not neglect. For the enabler analysis, you could incorporate verbatim comments from your partner to add flavour to the write-ups. These will help you to clarify the enablers within each organisation and to understand the reasons behind the process performance gaps.

At the end of the data-collection stage, the benchmarking team should prepare two reports: a *working report* and an *executive report*. Both reports should focus on the practices, existing or proposed, which offer opportunities for improvement. The result will be documents that will support your process by setting improvement goals and selecting specific opportunities. These will be the changes in practices and the supporting enablers that are required in your unique organisation.

The working report will be an extensive 'living' document for the benchmarking team. This will support the team as it moves into the analysis stage. The report should contain:

- All site-visit reports
- Tabulations of metric and practice data
- A gap analysis
- Process-improvement recommendations

The executive report will be a summary document that will include the key findings from the visits and recommend the appropriate actions to be taken.

Summary

Today we have been through the data-collection stage of the benchmarking roadmap. It may have surprised the reader that conducting the site visit was not the major activity in this stage. The site visit is an activity that has to be put into context with all the rest of the preparation that must be carried out prior to execution.

Now that all our data is collected and the reports are complete, we can look forward to Friday when we shall be analysing the data and implementing the improvement recommendations.

Analysing and using the data

Today we start by analysing the data or knowledge we have collected. Then we will examine the issues involved in using the data to adapt our current practices. These are the final two steps on the benchmarking roadmap outlined on page 31.

The main tasks in analysing the data, which we will discuss today, are as follows:

- Normalise the performance data
- Construct a comparison matrix
- Identify the best practices
- Isolate the involved process enablers

Normalising the performance data

Before comparing the data, you must make sure that you will be 'comparing apples with apples'. This is achieved by *normalising* the data.

The following figure gives the details of a study of retail stores. In this figure the data has been normalised for 'Revenue per employee' and 'Revenue per store'. As can be seen from the figure, many extra questions could be asked such as 'How many employees are there per store?', 'How big are the stores?' and 'What is the average value of the merchandise sold?'. It is important that the comparisons are made on a fair basis. Common normalisation factors include size, age and economy.

	Revenue per employee	Revenue per store (millions)
Store A	£148,523	£22
Store B	£148,000	£26
Store C	£110,323	£48
Store D	£103,110	£9
Store E	£91,429	£17

Constructing a comparison matrix

We are now in a position to compare the data from several sources and it can be very helpful at this stage to present this in matrix form.

The comparison matrix will be different for every study since every study is unique. Most of the data required to complete the matrix will be available in the site-visit report. It is not intended that all the information in the report be transferred to the matrix as the matrix represents only a summary for comparison purposes.

A comparisom matrix will include the various companies on the horizontal axis and the following elements, each of which we will discuss in turn, on the vertical axis:

- The study subject
- The business profile
- The environment/culture
- Organisational results
- Study measures

The study subject
The study subject should be stated together with a long-term study reference number.

The business profile
Record all the key facts about the organisation that need to be taken into account in the comparison.

The environment/culture
During the site visit, the benchmarking team will have formed a view of the degree of maturity – as reflected, for example, in its communication culture – of the organisation. These views can be summarised and recorded here.

Organisational results
Although the study may have been addressing only a small-scope topic, it is still useful to record the overall level of performance of the organisation – preferably as measured against the European Business Excellence Model. These results will indicate the degree of business excellence of the company.

Study measures
In this section the benchmarking team will record the measures that were identified on Wednesday at the end of the 'Planning the study' stage. It would also be of value for comparison purposes to summarise the key practices behind the measurement results, together with the actual performance level both for your own company and for your benchmarking partners. As a guideline, you should set the level of detail high enough to highlight significant steps but without descending into minute detail.

Comparing the results of your company over varying processes side by side with those of your benchmarking partners is a very powerful tool. The figure below illustrates the results of a benchmarking study into the time taken for doctors to treat patients in the casualty departments of different hospitals.

Study measure	Own hospital	Hospital A	Hospital B	Hospital C
First contact on entering casualty department	00:04:00	00:08:30	00:08:30	00:00:30
Patient enters treatment room	00:28:00	01:07:00	00:12:45	00:15:30
Doctor begins treatment	00:41:00	01:24:00	00:48:00	00:29:00
Number of annual casualty visits	44,000	52,500	44,000	36,500
Average number of visits per day per doctor	60	72	81	67

Study subject: minimising the time taken to process a patient (cycle time)

This study clearly shows that Hospital C gives the best overall service. However, this is not true for all steps in the process: the patient actually enters the treatment room faster at Hospital B (although they do then wait there a longer time than at Hospital C).

A word of warning. This analysis of data is not yet a firm base for adapting one's own processes. These figures have only produced some guidelines to help identify best practices. We may need more information, for example on what kind of patients were involved and what level of information they obtained from their GP.

Identifying the best practices

The key to the comparison matrix lies in the discovery of those practices that are driving the numbers. By comparing the results and the summary practices side by side, the benchmarking team should be able to generate a shortlist of best practices. The team can then analyse these further with a view to adapting them for their own organisation.

Practices and enablers
Before moving on, we should clarify the difference between *practices* and *enablers:*

- Practices are the operations that make up the process
- Enablers are the activities that facilitate the implementation of a best practice

Improvement goals are achieved through changing practices. So for example, if we have a goal to decrease the response time for customer complaints, we will consider the:

- Practice of the use of the centralised database for customer complaints
- Enabler for that practice, which here is the complaints-logging system

How exactly best practices are identified will depend on the particular subject under study. The general criteria to be looked for, however, are as follows:

- What is the impact of the practice on the business?
- How easy is it to implement?
- Are the results near-term or long-term?
- Are the results tactical or strategic in nature?
- Do the results tie directly to a specified goal or priority?
- Do the results give only a moderate or a major leverage on those priorities?
- Are the results controllable?
- Do the practices complement other initiatives and activities already under way?

Isolating the involved process enablers

The final task in the data-analysis stage is to determine the process enablers for the identified best practices. Several best practices will have been identified, and so this analysis must be repeated for each one. The most popular way to do this is to use the Fishbone or Ishikawa diagram. This is also known as a 'Cause and Effect' diagram, though not in the normal sense since 'Effect' here means 'Best Practice' and 'Cause' means 'Enablers'. The figure below illustrates the use of this tool.

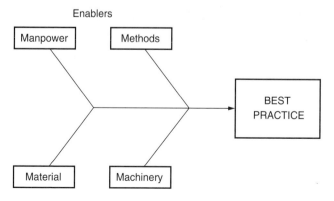

The benchmarking team will use this diagram in brainstorming sessions to identify both the enablers and the best practices to be used in the next stage of the benchmarking road map on page 31: 'Adapt'.

Adapting the best practices and enablers

Successful implementation will be dependent on two things. These are:

- Support from upper management and process stakeholders
- An organised strategy with realistic, actionable improvement goals

The key steps in the 'Adapt' stage are:

- Communicate findings and gain a commitment to change
- Set goals to close the gaps
- Adapt the enablers
- Develop the implementation plan and implement it
- Monitor and report on progress

Communicating findings and gaining a commitment to change

People tend not to like change, especially change that on the surface appears to be inconvenient. To ensure the success of the current benchmarking projects, as well as future projects, it is therefore imperative to communicate specific benchmarking findings throughout the duration of the project so that it sinks in that change is coming. Even if you do have support from senior management for the change, there may be resistance from lower organisational levels. Typically, this resistance to change stems from fear: fear of losing jobs, status, control, resources and familiarity. So how do you gain support? The best way is to conduct a *stakeholder analysis* to identify potential resistance and then address these concerns.

Setting goals to close the gaps

Goals need to be set for an implementation plan. You will recall that during the internal-analysis stage, data was collected on current and past performance. The present step is where we now use that data. The first diagram below shows the situation where your organisation's performance is compared against the benchmark. The gap in performance is clear, and the resulting improvement goals are illustrated in the second diagram.

Current performance compared to benchmark

Predicting future performance

There is one word of caution in setting improvement goals. Benchmarks may be used for understanding the current best performance achievements, and they will be valuable for setting short-term goals or gaining commitments to improved levels of near-term performance. These same benchmarks are not, however, valid for long-term use since the projections of future potential performance may not always follow the historical model.

Improvement processes may result in either continuous incremental gains (Kaisen) or strategic breakthroughs that leapfrog the competition (Hoshin). You must remain alert for both these types of improvement potential. Many of the latter, breakthrough improvements come from changing the business paradigm or from significant technological developments.

Adapting the enablers

When we analysed the best practices earlier today to come up with a list of key enablers, we considered *all* enablers, including our own. If an organisation wants to achieve the same level of performance as the benchmark organisation, then it could choose to copy the enablers and practices found in that organisation.

The secret in using benchmarking to achieve breakthrough change is to synthesise key actions, taken after a consideration of all the information available, to come up with innovative approaches. One part of the thought process involved is to consider the environment of the enabler and how well it will work in your own organisation. This thought process can be aided by the use of two tools:

- The adaptability check
- The force field analysis

In the adaptability check, a list is made of all the issues surrounding the transfer of the enabler into your organisation. There are three broad factors involved here:

1 process considerations
2 current business practices
3 the organisational structure

You will be interested in the things that *prevent* the successful transfer of the enabler as well as in the things that will aid its transfer. So for example, if it is a current business practice to train 'on the job' but the enabler calls for 'off the job' training, then this could be a barrier to implementation. The output from the adaptability check can be used in conjunction with the second tool, the *force field analysis*.

The force field analysis is used to both identify those things that will *help* the implementation of the new practices and those things that will act as *barriers*. To conduct this analysis, the benchmarking team will transfer the data generated in the adaptability check to a chart similar to that shown below. All the things that stand *in favour of* the change are written on one side of the chart – in this example, the left-hand side – and all the things that are *opposing* the change are written on the other side. Against each item a line is drawn representing the strength of the particular force. The object of the exercise is to plan actions that will *strengthen* the positive forces and *weaken* the negative ones and thus result in a 'shift' of the centre line towards the left.

The output from the force field analysis will be used in the next stage when the benchmarking team develops the *implementation plan*.

Developing the implementation plan and implementing it

The implementation plan is where the benchmarking team pulls all relevant actions together. This plan should cover the adaptation of all the practices and enablers. These should be broken down into specific activity steps. One way of constructing an implementation plan is to use a 'Gantt Chart'. This universal project-planning tool is covered in detail in project-management books, and several computer programmes are available to help you to construct one.

The implementation plan can be produced as a *summary sheet* (illustrated overleaf), supplemented with an *activity list* covering all the performance targets and milestones. Implementation can now proceed.

Process studied:			
Related Critical Success Factor:			
Process owner:		Date:	
Benchmarking team members:			
Objective of study:			
Summary of study results:			
Benchmarks observed			
Measure	Our performance	Benchmark	Benchmark company
Short-term goals Date		Long-term goals Date	

Benchmarking implementation plan summary sheet

Monitoring and reporting on progress

Once the implementation plan has been developed and
signed off and implementation has started, it is important
to monitor and report on progress concerning the actions
and milestones. The most effective way to do this is by

getting the implementation-plan actions onto the agenda of the business-planning reviews: since the need for the study originally came from a *strategic* need, it is logical for the review to take place in this forum. In addition, these reviews will be attended by senior management, and so the implementation of the study recommendations will succeed in gaining their attention also.

Summary

Today we have seen how you analyse the data and adopt the findings of the study so as to come up with an implementation plan. In doing so we have now completed our run-through of the benchmarking roadmap, and we have completed our benchmarking study.

Tomorrow we go on to discuss some other aspects of benchmarking, including conducting an assessment of your own benchmarking studies that will enable you to improve their effectiveness.

Maintaining leadership

Benchmarking is a *journey*, not a destination; a *process*, not a tool; and a *means*, not an end. Unfortunately, the world does not stand still and you have to work to stay ahead.

Once a benchmarking study has been completed, the results should be logged on the internal benchmarking database. This database should have the facility to draw your attention to the studies at a regular interval so that their status can be reviewed. Periodically, benchmarks will have to be recalibrated and studies recycled. The objective of recalibration is to maintain and update current benchmarks to ensure that they are continuously based upon the best methods and practices. Recalibration is a *proactive* process.

Rapid benchmarking

Some organisations become frustrated at the time it takes to conduct a benchmarking study. This frustration is usually shown by the more experienced benchmarking organisations, and it has led these organisations to develop 'rapid benchmarking' techniques.

The concept of rapid benchmarking was born when John Hendrick, benchmarking expert for AT&T Global Business Communications Systems, questioned how the value of benchmarking could be measured. He concluded that the value added by benchmarking was a function of the value of the comparative-performance data generated or the key learnings uncovered – or both – considered against the time taken to carry out the study. And his view was that if benchmarking is to survive, methods must be found that enable the key learnings to be uncovered *faster*.

AT&T define 'rapid benchmarking' as:

> a 60–90 day benchmarking project management template for experienced process teams to compare their process metrics and current process performance to best performers

The reasons for developing rapid benchmarking within AT&T were quite straightforward. They found that the longer it took to complete a benchmarking project, the more difficult it became to sustain enthusiasm and support within the organisation. In addition, the longer it took teams to consolidate benchmarking findings into a set of recommendations, the greater the expectation that *significant* findings would be made. AT&T termed these last two factors the 'investment mentality'. They also observed that best-in-the-class company research and the establishment of industry-information-sharing relationships often consumed over 50% of a benchmarking project's time. Finally, many teams chose benchmarking partners on the basis of secondary information or a consultant's recommendation.

How to assess your benchmarking efforts

Companies within Europe and America are recognised as being world class in the area of business excellence thanks to the respective European Quality Award and Malcolm Baldrige Award procedures. For benchmarking alone, the annual American Productivity and Quality Center's (APQC's) Benchmarking Awards are available. These Benchmarking Awards recognise benchmarking excellence and provide a platform for those with excellent examples of benchmarking to disseminate their knowledge and further the improvement of organisations.

The purposes of the above awards are fourfold. They are to:

- Showcase best practices
- Recognise excellence
- Set standards for processes and results
- Provide criteria for self-assessments

The APCQ's scheme comprises three categories of award: the Benchmarking Research Award, the Benchmarking Study Award and the Award for Excellence in Benchmarking.

It is not our intention to discuss the above awards or the award process itself in detail – more information can be obtained by reading *Assessing Business Excellence* by Porter and Tanner, University of Bradford Management Centre, 1996. Our main reason for drawing your attention to the awards is that one of them, the Benchmarking Study Award, can be used by you as a checklist to improve your benchmarking efforts. Summaries of award-winning entries are available from the APQC (see the address on page 25) so that you can learn from other companies' approaches to benchmarking.

The scoring for awards is achieved by comparing the element that is being scored against a *matrix*. The matrix example illustrated on the following pages is a simplified

version of that used for the American Malcolm Baldrige
Award:

Score	Approach/deployment	Results
0%	• Anecdotal information • No systematic approach evident in the information presented	• No data reported, or anecdotal data only • Data not responsive to the major requirements of the item
10% to 30%	• The beginning of a systematic approach to addressing the primary purposes of the item • Significant gaps still exist in deployment that would inhibit progress in achieving the major purposes of the item	• Early states of developing data • Some improvement-trend data or early good performance reported • No data reported for many to most areas of importance to the item • Data not reported for the organisation's key performance-related business factors
40% to 60%	• A sound systematic approach, responsive to the primary purposes of the item • A fact-based process in place in key areas addressed by the item • No major gaps in deployment, though some components may still be in early stages of deployment	• Improvements or good performance trends reported in key areas of importance both to the item requirements and to the study or organisation's key performance-related business factors • Some trends or current performance, or both, can be evaluated against relevant comparisons, benchmarks or levels
70% to 90%	• A sound systematic approach responsive to the overall purposes of the item • A fact-based improvement process, acting as a key management tool • Evidence of innovation	• Good to excellent improvement trends in most key areas of importance, both to the item requirements and to the study or organisation's key performance-related business factors, or sustained good to excellent performance in those areas

Score	Approach/deployment	Results
		• Many to most trends and current performance can be evaluated against world-class comparisons, benchmarks or levels • Current performance is good to excellent in most areas of importance, both to the item requirements and to the study or organisation's key performance-related business factors and processes
100%	• A sound systematic approach, fully responsive to the primary purposes of the item • The approach is fully deployed without weaknesses or gaps in any areas • Very strong refinement and integration, backed by excellent analysis • High levels of innovation and deployment	• Excellent improvement trends in most to all key areas of importance, both to the item requirements and to the company's key performance-related business factors, or sustained excellent performance in these areas • Most to all trends and current performance can be evaluated against world-class comparisons, benchmarks or levels • Current performance is excellent in most areas of importance, both to the item requirements and to the study or organisation's key performance-related business factors • Strong evidence of process and benchmark leadership demonstrated

Note: Scores are in increments of 10%
Source: American Productivity and Quality Center

A company new to benchmarking would be likely to score between 0 and 100 points out of a total of 300 at their first assessment, and even a world-class company would only manage around 250 points, so the current assessment standard is extremely tough.

If an assessment is carried out on a regular basis, you should see a gradual improvement in your organisation's score. The greatest value of an assessment is that it enables you to discover areas for improvement, which in turn will enable you to improve your benchmarking efforts.

Summary

Today we have considered the following:

- Maintaining and updating the database
- Continuous self-assessment
- Benchmarking and improvement awards
- Pitfalls and temptations in benchmarking

Conclusion

This week we have seen that benchmarking requires a strong degree of commitment – from management and from all others involved. It takes time and resources. It needs a disciplined and systematic approach. In short, it is not easy and it is not for the faint-hearted.

But then who has the right to believe that *aiming to be the best* should ever be easy?

The Lucky Baseball Bat

by Matt Christopher

Illustrated by Dee deRosa

LITTLE, BROWN AND COMPANY

New York ⌇ An AOL Time Warner Company

The Lucky
Baseball Bat

First Paperback Edition

This is a revised edition of *The Lucky Baseball Bat* published in
1954 by Little, Brown and Company.

The characters and events portrayed in this book are fictitious.
Any similarity to real persons, living or dead, is coincidental
and not intended by the author.

Matt Christopher® is a registered trademark of
Catherine M. Christopher.

Christopher, Matt.
    The lucky baseball bat / by Matt Christopher ; illustrated
by Dee deRosa. — Rev. ed.
    p.   cm. —
    Summary: When Martin loses his lucky baseball bat, and
his confidence along with it, he wonders if he will recover both
in
time to help the tigers win the championship.

    ISBN 0-316-14260-3 (pb)
    [1. Baseball — Fiction.   2. Self-confidence — Fiction.
I. deRosa, Dee, ill.   II. Title.
PZ7.C458Lu 1991
[E] — dc20   90-19188

PB: 20   19   18   17   16   15   14   13

COM-MO

PRINTED IN THE UNITED STATES OF AMERICA

To Marty, Pam, Dale, and Duane

1

Martin bit his lip and wiped his damp
forehead with the back of his hand. His
younger sister, Jeannie, scowled at him.

"What're you afraid of? Go in there and
ask them," she said.

"Ask who?" Martin said.

He looked at the group of boys scattered on
the ball field. They were practicing, throwing
the ball among themselves to limber up their
muscles and get the feel of it.

Jeannie brushed a tangle of curly hair away from her eyes and pointed. "Ask that man there. Jim Cassell. He's the coach, I think."

Martin didn't want to ask Jim Cassell. Mr. Cassell might tell him to go home. He didn't know Martin, and Martin didn't know him. That was the trouble. Martin knew hardly anybody here. They had just moved into the city.

"I think I'll just go out there with those kids and see if they'll throw a ball to me," he said. "That'll be all right, won't it?"

Jeannie nodded. "Go ahead. Maybe it's the best way."

Martin ran slowly toward the scattered group of boys. They were all about his age, some a little smaller, some taller. Most of them had baseball gloves. He wished he had one. You didn't look like a baseball player without a baseball glove.

All at once he heard Coach Cassell yell:

"Okay, boys! Spread out! A couple of you get in center field!"

The boys scampered into different positions, but Martin didn't move from the position he'd taken in left field. Coach Cassell was having the boys start batting practice. A tall, skinny kid stood on the mound. He pitched the ball twice. Each time, the boy at bat swung at the ball and missed.

The third time he connected. Martin heard the sharp *crack!* It was followed by a scramble of feet not far behind him. He looked up, and sure enough the ball, looking like a small white pill, was curving through the air in his direction!

"I got it! I got it!" he cried. He forgot that he had no glove. His sneakers slipped on the short-cut grass as he tried to get in position under the ball.

Somebody bumped into him, but he didn't give ground. "I got it!" he yelled again.

The ball came directly at him, and he reached for it with both hands. In the next instant the hurtling ball became a blur, and he felt it slide through his hands and strike solidly against his chest.

Missed it!

"Nice catch!" a boy sneered. "Where did you learn to play ball?"

2

_____

"For Pete's sake!" the coach yelled. "Don't try to catch a ball without a glove! You'll get hurt!"

Martin looked at his bare hands, feeling his heart pound in his chest. He turned and walked away, sticking his hands in his pockets. "Come on," he said when he reached Jeannie. "Let's go home."

"Sure," Jeannie agreed. "You can do something else besides play baseball!"

"But I don't want to do anything else!" Martin said angrily. "I want to play baseball!"

"Hello!" a voice cut in as Martin and Jeannie started to walk off the field. "What's the matter, kid? You look as if you've lost your best friend."

Martin looked around at a tall, dark-haired boy standing behind them. "Nothing's the matter," he answered. He kept walking, his heels scraping the dirt and pebbles.

"Hey, wait a minute!" the tall stranger called after them. "You didn't answer me. What happened? Won't they let you play ball with them?"

"I haven't got a glove," Martin explained. "I'm sure I could catch those balls if I had a glove."

The tall boy laughed in a friendly way. "Tell you what," he said. "My name's Barry Welton. I live around the corner on Grant Street, to the right."

"We live a block to the left," Jeannie said warmly. "I'm Jeannie Allan, and this is my brother Martin."

"Glad to meet you. Now come on." He made a motion with his hand and began to walk toward Grant Street.

"Where are you going?" Martin asked.

"To my house. I'm going to give you something. Something I think you'd like to have."

When they reached Barry's house, a gray wood-frame building with yellow shutters, he asked them to wait in the living room while he ran upstairs. A few seconds later he was back, and Martin's eyes almost bugged out of his head.

Barry was carrying a bat and a glove!

"Here." He grinned. "These are yours. Now maybe they'll let you play. Okay?"

"Wow!" Martin cried. "You're giving these to me?"

"Right! I've had that glove ever since I was your size, and I outgrew that bat years ago. It was a lucky bat for me. Maybe it'll be a lucky one for you, too."

"Wow!" said Martin again, his heart thumping excitedly. "Thanks! Thanks a lot, Barry!" He turned to his sister. "Come on, Jeannie! Let's go back to the park!"

The kids were still having batting practice. Martin had Jeannie hang on to the bat while he put on the glove and ran out to the field. Two of the boys saw him with the glove and said something to each other. He acted as if he didn't see them. He didn't care what they said. He had as much right to be here as they did.

Suddenly he saw Jim Cassell gazing toward the outfield. The coach seemed to be looking directly at him, and Martin's heart fell.

"Kid!" the coach yelled at him. "Move over a little — toward center field!"

A thrill of excitement went through him as he ran over to a spot between left and center fields. The coach had given him an order as if he were already a member of the team! He almost prayed a ball would come his way. He had not caught a ball since last summer, but he knew how to do it. Maybe he could even show the kids a thing or two!

And then, even while he was thinking about it, he saw a ball hit out his way. The closer of the two boys covering center field came running for it, shouting at the top of his lungs, "I've got it! I've got it!"

Martin knew it was his ball more than the other boy's. He needed to take only four or five steps backward. He reached up — and tried to out-yell the other boy.

"It's mine! Let it go! It's mine!"

"Let him take it, Tommy!" Coach Cassell's voice boomed from near home plate.

Martin felt a shoulder hit his arm. It threw him off balance enough so that the ball struck the fingers of his glove and slipped right through. *Bang!* On his chest again, barely missing his throat. The ball dropped to the grass and bounced away.

Martin turned, tears choking him. He saw

that the other fielder was the same boy who had made a nasty remark earlier.

"So it's you again," the boy said. "With a glove, too!" He laughed. "Even with a glove you miss them. Why don't you go home and stay there? We don't want any hicks on this team!"

3

This time when Martin and Jeannie went home, there was no Barry Welton around. Martin was glad Barry had not seen how foolish he had looked on the diamond.

"I'm glad you're home, kids," their mother said. "We're almost ready for supper."

Then she caught sight of the bat and glove Martin was carrying. "Where on earth did you get those?" she asked.

"A nice guy named Barry Welton gave them to me," Martin said, then told his mother what had happened.

The basement door opened and Martin's tall, husky father came in. He stared at the bat and glove, too, and Martin had to tell all about it again. He left out one thing, though. He didn't tell them he was going to give the bat and glove back to Barry.

After supper Martin and Jeannie cleared the table and put the dishes in the dishwasher. For a minute Martin got to thinking about his sister. If only she liked baseball, moving to the city would have been easier. They could play together and hang out like pals. Then it wouldn't matter so much that the other kids wouldn't let him play. But Jeannie always got bored whenever Martin tried to teach her to play. Maybe things would be different when she was older, Martin thought as he walked out onto the front porch.

All at once he heard the slap of sneakers on the sidewalk. It was Barry Welton.

"Hi, Barry!" he called.

"Hi, Marty," Barry answered. "Taking it easy?"

Martin nodded. "Wait a minute, Barry," he said. "I'll be right back." Martin ran into the house.

He got the bat and glove and brought them out. "Here," he said, swallowing a lump in his throat. "Take them back. They'll never let me play baseball around here!"

Barry frowned, but then a grin came over his face. "Hey, kid. Don't go acting like that or you'll never play ball! Got a ball?"

Martin said, "Yeah, but —"

"Get it. We'll play a little catch."

Martin went inside again, full of excitement this time, and got the ball.

"Let's go out to the side of the house," Barry suggested, "so we won't be throwing toward the windows."

Martin thrilled at the expert way Barry caught the balls, pulling his hands down and away with the ball. He tried to do the same. They played catch for about fifteen minutes, and then Barry said he had to go. In the meantime Jeannie had come out to jump rope on the porch. After Barry left, Martin still wanted to play.

"Jeannie," Martin said, "how about throwing the ball to me in the backyard? I'll bat. Then after a while you can bat."

"Okay."

Martin was grateful that she was willing, even though she didn't like baseball that much. She wasn't such a bad sister after all.

They had more room in the backyard. But it was not as much fun as Martin had hoped. Each time Jeannie threw the ball, he swung and missed.

At first he joked with Jeannie about throwing him wild pitches. But then missing the ball four, five, six times in a row got under his skin. He was growing warm all over, and he

knew it was because he was getting anxious and mad.

"Martin," said Jeannie, "what's the matter? Can't you even hit it?"

"I could if you threw it right!" Martin said angrily.

"Well, who wants to play this boring game, anyway?" Jeannie yelled back. She threw the ball down in the dirt.

Martin threw his bat down, too.

They heard Mom's voice calling from the house: "Jeannie! Martin!"

They ran into the kitchen. Their mother held the keys to the car in her hand.

"If you two can sit in the backseat without fighting, maybe we could take a trip to the movies," she said.

"Yeah!" They said it almost together, their faces lighting up like Fourth-of-July sparklers.

"Okay," she said. "Get washed and dressed."

The movie was a comedy. They laughed all

the way through it. Not once did Martin think about baseball.

Martin was in bed before he remembered the bat he had left outside. He rushed out the side door and searched all around the spot where he was sure he had left it. But it was nowhere around.

The bat was gone!

4

First thing the next morning, Martin searched the backyard again. The bat could have rolled behind one of Dad's rosebushes, or into the higher grass that grew close to the wire fence, he thought. But he still could not find it.

Martin felt sick. He would not have minded so much except that the bat was a gift from Barry. And now it was gone. What could have happened to it? Did somebody take it?

He couldn't stop thinking about the bat as he wandered up the street. Then he saw some boys playing with a tennis ball. One of them was Rick Savora.

Rick was about eleven or twelve — bigger than Martin. He stood with his legs spread apart and held a bat on his shoulder, waiting for another boy to pitch him the tennis ball. Farther down the street was a third boy, waiting to chase the ball in case Rick hit it.

Martin waited to see what Rick would do. Rick, he remembered, was one of the boys at the park yesterday. He looked as if he might be the best player of them all.

Rick swung at the ball and hit it down the street past the pitcher. He dropped the bat and raced around the squares of cardboard they were using for bases.

Then Martin noticed the bat. It had rolled a little way as Rick had thrown it and then had stopped. Martin's heart pounded like mad. He started to walk down the street.

One of the boys saw him. "Here comes that Allan kid!" he cried out.

Rick stood on second, his hands on his knees. When he heard the boy shout, he rose and scowled at Martin.

"What do you want?" he yelled.

Martin didn't answer. He looked at Rick and then again at the bat. The more he looked at it, the more it looked like the one Barry had given him.

The boys muttered in low tones among themselves. One of them walked off the street. Rick picked up the cardboard piece that was second base, got the bat, and walked off the street, too. The catcher followed him.

All three gave Martin dirty looks and went up on the porch of a red brick house nearby.

A hurt look crept into Martin's eyes, and an ache filled his throat, wanting to turn into tears. He spun on his heel and ran all the way home.

He met Jeannie in front of the house, bouncing a rubber ball up and down on the sidewalk.

"Rick Savora's got my bat!" Martin exclaimed.

Jeannie's eyes widened. "Did you ask him for it?"

"No. I didn't have a chance. He and some other kids went into his house when they saw me coming."

Jeannie's lips tightened. "Let's go to his house and ask him for that bat," she said, determined.

"What if he won't give it to me?" Martin asked.

"Then we'll tell Dad about it."

Martin shook his head. "No. I won't tell Dad anything. I don't want the kids to think I'm a baby."

"Well, let's go anyway. If it's your bat, he must have stolen it, and we'll make him give it back."

Together they walked to Rick Savora's house. Rick answered Martin's knock. He scowled when he saw who his callers were.

"You were playing with my baseball bat," Martin said. "I want it back."

"You're crazy!" Rick snapped. "I haven't got your bat!"

"Yes, you have. You were playing with it on the street just a little while ago. I saw it."

Rick's eyes blazed with anger. "Just a minute!" he snarled.

He went inside and soon returned with a small yellow bat.

"There! Is that your bat?"

Martin looked at it closely. "No," he said. "But that isn't the one you were playing with."

"You're crazy!" Rick said again. "You must've been seeing things!"

He slammed the door so hard the wood panels shook. Jeannie and Martin turned and stared at each other.

"He's lying," Martin said as they started back up the street. "I know he's lying!"

5

A little after dinnertime, Martin was sitting on the porch when a car stopped in front of the house. "Hey, son!" called the driver. "Want to come to the park and play ball?"

Martin recognized Coach Jim Cassell. He walked slowly down the porch steps and toward the car.

Then he saw Rick Savora sitting in the car next to Mr. Cassell. Rick didn't look at him.

Martin felt a tightening in his chest. "I — I don't think so," he said. "I don't think I want to play baseball."

"What? I thought you *wanted* to play."

Martin shrugged. He didn't want to say that he wouldn't play because Rick was on the team. He couldn't tell the coach that Rick had stolen his bat and then lied about it.

Coach Cassell flashed a smile. "Got a glove?"

Martin nodded. "Yes."

"Then get it. We're going to have a team in the Grasshoppers League, and since you're one of the boys in the neighborhood, maybe we'll have room for you on the team."

"A Grasshoppers League?" He frowned. "What's that?"

"A league we have here. There are six teams in it. Each team plays two games a week during the summer vacation. The winning team gets a free banquet and goes to see a World Series game. It's something worth shooting for. Don't you think so?"

"WOW!" Martin's face brightened. "I'll say it is!"

The coach's smile broadened. "Now you want to come along?"

"You bet! Wait! I'll run in and get my glove!"

At the field, Coach Cassell had two of the tallest boys choose sides. Rick Savora chose for one side, and a red-haired boy named Lennie Moore chose for the other. Lennie picked Martin for his team. Then the coach flipped a quarter to see whose side would bat first. Rick called "heads" and won the toss. He chose to bat last.

Coach Cassell told the boys which positions they were to play, then called out the hitters for Lennie's team. Martin noticed that Rick was playing shortstop. He wondered what position the coach would let him play. He had never thought about playing in a league! And to have a chance to see a World Series game! What a wonderful thing that would be! Even his parents had never seen a World Series game!

"Okay, Martin! Your turn to bat!"

He sprang from the bench, surprised that his name was called so soon. The second one!

He picked up one of the bats and went to the plate. His heart hammered. He got into position beside the plate, tapped it a couple of times with the bat, and waited for the pitcher to throw. The next thing Martin saw was the ball coming at him and over the plate.

He swung. Missed!

Coach Cassell was acting as umpire. "Strike!" he said. Then he turned to Martin: "Get a little closer to the plate, Martin. You're too far from it. And keep your feet farther apart."

Martin tried to do what the coach said. Again he waited for the pitch. He swung! Missed again!

Sweat beaded on his forehead. He was growing more nervous by the second. If he didn't get a hit, they would see he wasn't any good. And then they wouldn't want him on the team.

The third pitch came in. He had to hit it

now. He was thinking that if he had his own bat, the one Barry had given him, it would have been a cinch. This bat was too heavy.

The ball was in there, straight as an arrow. Chest-high. He swung!

He heard the ball hit the catcher's mitt. The bat, following through on his swing, spun him almost all the way around.

"Strike three!" said Coach Cassell.

6

The day of the first game in the Grasshoppers League came quickly. Too quickly for Martin. He dreaded having to play in front of a crowd. In every practice he had been hardly able to hit the ball.

His dad had given him a pep talk. He had even taken him to a professional game, to show him that even major leaguers strike out sometimes.

But it didn't make Martin feel much better. What he really needed was his own bat back.

He was sure that with his own bat he would hit.

Martin's team, the Tigers, was playing the Indians. Coach Cassell put Martin out in left field — because Martin was good at catching fly balls, he said.

The Tigers were up first, and Kenny Stokes was the leadoff batter. He hit the second pitch for a blooping fly to the shortstop.

Then Martin walked to the plate. The bat felt heavy in his hands. He hadn't been able to find one among the team's bats that fitted him as well as the one Barry had given him.

The pitch came in, but he wasn't ready for it. He let it go by. "Strike!" yelled the umpire.

"Come on, Martin!" He heard the coach's voice from the bench. "Hit it when it's in there!"

He ticked the next one. It went sailing back over the catcher's shoulder, striking the backstop screen.

"You're feeling it!" he heard the coach shout.

He got ready for the third pitch. With an 0 and 2 count on him he was in a tough spot. He wished the coach had not put him second in the batting order. Everybody would expect too much from him.

The pitcher wound up, then threw. But the ball came in too wide. Martin let it go by.

"Ball!" said the umpire.

Now the count was one ball, two strikes. He felt a little better. Again the pitch. It came in straight and a little low, but Martin swung at it. And missed!

"Strike three!" boomed the umpire.

Martin dropped the bat and walked sadly back to the bench. He knew what everybody was thinking.

Jackie Barnes was up next. He hit the ball to the left of second base for a single. Rick Savora followed him and hit the first pitch for

a double. Next, Chuck Sterns hit a grounder through short, scoring Jackie and Rick. Then Chuck got out trying to steal second.

When the Indians came to bat, they scored three runs, edging ahead of the Tigers, 3 to 2.

Larry Munson was on second base when Martin came to bat again. It was the third inning. If he got a hit now, Larry might score to tie the game.

The pitch came in. It was a little high, but it didn't look bad. Martin cut at it. *Crack!* The ball looked as big as a balloon as it floated through the air toward the pitcher. Martin threw down the bat and started running slowly toward first.

"Run, Martin!" Coach Cassell shouted. "Run!"

But the ball dropped into the pitcher's hands. Sadly, Martin turned and headed back for the bench.

Nobody said anything to him, but he heard the coach say, "Artie, play catch with somebody. You're going in in place of Martin next inning." He looked up at Martin. "Martin —"

"I heard you, Coach," Martin said. Then he turned to Rick, his eyes hard as steel.

"If you'd give my bat back to me, I could hit that ball!" he cried bitterly. "You're a thief, that's what you are! You stole my bat!"

7

Rick's face paled, and his mouth opened as if he were going to say something. But Martin was already running off the field, carrying his glove.

He wondered what Jeannie and his mother and father would say when he came home early. Well, what could they say? They could see that he couldn't hit the ball. It was only right that he had been taken out.

He saw a fat, chubby-legged little boy run out into the street, chasing after a blue-and-red rubber ball. He wasn't more than three years old.

A car whizzed around the corner, its tires screaming on the pavement. Martin stared at the car, then at the little boy. Terror took hold of him. The little boy wasn't paying any attention to the car!

Suddenly the loud cry of a woman reached Martin's ears. "Gary! Gary, get back here! Watch that car!"

There was fear in her voice. Martin saw her run toward the street. "Gary!" she screamed again.

The little boy did not move. Realizing that the car would not be able to stop in time, Martin sprinted out into the street, picked up the boy, and snatched him out of the way.

The car's brakes squealed, its tires leaving twin black marks on the street behind it. Then it stopped, and a man looked out of the window, his face ghost-white.

"Man!" he exclaimed. "That was close!"

"It sure was!" said Martin with a shudder. The little boy started to cry, and Martin carried him to his mother. He saw that their backyard faced his backyard.

"Thank you!" the boy's mother said to Martin. "Thank you so much!" Her face was white as she bent and picked up her little son.

Then a tall, brown-haired man ran out of the house, followed by a freckle-faced boy, a year or two younger than Martin, who Martin recognized as Freckles Ginty. Shakily, the woman told her husband what had happened. The husband looked at Martin.

"That was quick thinking, son," he said. "We're very grateful to you for going after little Gary like that. You deserve some kind of reward."

Martin smiled. "That's all right," he said. "I'm glad I came by when I did."

He went home, feeling good at the man's words.

He had hardly been home five minutes when a soft knock sounded on the door. He knew it wasn't Dad or Mom. They wouldn't knock.

Wondering, he went to the door and opened it. It was Freckles Ginty. He held a bat in his hand, and he lifted it up to Martin.

Martin's eyes went wide. It was his missing bat!

8

At the ball field the next afternoon, just before practice, Martin approached Rick. He felt nervous and ashamed.

"Rick, I — I'm sorry that I said you had my bat. I got it back yesterday. Freckles Ginty had taken it out of my yard."

Rick frowned. "Why?"

"No good reason. He just saw it there and took it. Anyway, he brought it back and apologized."

Rick shrugged his shoulders. "Okay. You got it back. Maybe you can hit that ball now."

Martin heard the sarcasm in his voice and wondered if he and Rick would ever be friends. Rick was tough in a way, but everybody seemed to like him.

"Did you go in their house?" Rick said suddenly.

"No."

"You should see some of the things Mr. Ginty makes out of wood. Have Freckles show you sometime."

"I will!" Martin smiled.

On Thursday afternoon they had another Grasshoppers League game, this time against the Bears. Martin took Artie's place in the third inning, and when it was time to bat he wasn't nervous anymore. The bat felt just right in his hands. He felt good. He waited for the pitcher's throw — and hit the very first pitch for a single!

The crowd yelled. He could hear Coach Cassell's voice: "Thataboy, Marty! I knew you could do it!"

In the sixth inning, an important moment came, with the score 8 to 6 in the Bears' favor. The bases were loaded. Martin was up to bat again. A hit could tie the score. A good long drive could win the ball game.

The pitcher stepped onto the mound, glanced at the runner on third, then threw. Martin swung.

Crack! Like a white bullet the ball shot over the shortstop's head. Martin dropped the bat and sprinted to first base. The ball hit the grass halfway between the left and center fielders. Both boys ran as fast as they could after it, but it bounced on beyond them!

One run scored! Two! Three! Then Martin crossed the plate. A home run!

Martin's hit had won the game: 10 to 8.

The bat was lucky, all right. Martin kept on

hitting the ball in every game. Coach Cassell placed him third in the batting order, just before Rick. At the end of their fifth game, Martin's batting average was .453 and Rick's .422. Barry Welton came to see Martin play whenever he wasn't playing himself. And of course, Jeannie and his mom and dad never missed a ball game.

He even got on Jerry Walker's cable TV sports program. How long had he played ball? Jerry asked him. What was his batting average? What did his mother and father think of his playing baseball?

Finally Jerry mentioned his bat. "Coach Cassell tells me you have a bat you won't let anybody else use," he said. "You must think a lot of that bat, Martin," he added, smiling.

"I sure do," Martin answered. "It's my lucky bat."

When August came, the Tigers and the Bears were tied for first place, and the boys were growing more excited by the day. They kept talking about the World Series game that they might see.

"We've got three more games to play," Coach Cassell said. "We must win two out of those three. If we win, we're in!"

They started playing the first of the three games. For the first two innings neither team scored. Then the Bears picked up two runs.

In the fourth inning the Tigers scored two runs to even it up. It stayed that way till the first half of the sixth. Larry was first batter and got a single, a nice one over first base. Kenny Stokes walked. Then Martin came up, and everybody cheered.

He swung at the first pitch. Missed! The next one was a ball. The third was in there. He swung hard and hit it — a neat single — but something terrible happened: the bat broke in two! He held one piece in his hand. The other piece was flying out across the ground toward third base!

9

Martin didn't know what to do. Without his bat he was sure everything would be the way it was before. He wouldn't be able to hit again, and the coach wouldn't let him play anymore.

There were only two games left to play. The Tigers had won one. They had to win one more. If they lost the next two games, their chance of seeing a World Series game was gone.

"It isn't the bat, son," his father said to him. "It's you. You've got it in your head that you can't hit with any other bat, but you're wrong. Just try again. Try again, Martin."

Martin wished that it would rain on Friday, the day of their next game. But it didn't.

The Tigers were up first. The first two batters flied out. Then Martin came to the plate. He took three cuts and struck out.

"Never mind that, Marty," the coach said. "You'll hit it the next time."

Martin didn't say anything. When the next time came, he would strike out again, he thought. The coach would find that out himself. Maybe he didn't believe the bat made a difference, but it did. There must be something about that bat. That he'd struck out his first time up with another bat proved it. How could anybody say it didn't?

The game ended 7 to 4 in the Bears' favor.

*　　　*　　　*

At one o'clock Saturday afternoon, Martin was still home. The game was scheduled to start at exactly one-thirty.

His father appeared at the living-room door. He frowned. "Martin! Why aren't you at the baseball field?"

Martin's heart started to pound. "I'm not going to the game," he said.

"Why not?"

"Because I'm no good. I can't hit. I can't field. The coach just lets me play because I *used* to be good."

"That's no way to talk, son," his father said. "The coach lets you play because he knows you're good. You're just thinking about that bat again. And you're wrong. I wish I could make you understand that."

The doorbell chimed and his dad went to answer it.

"Martin!" he called. "Someone to see you!"

Martin walked across the room to the door, then stopped. It was Freckles Ginty.

"Hello, Martin. I've got something for you."

From behind his back Freckles pulled a bat. Martin stared. It was exactly like the one he had broken!

His mouth fell open. "Where — where did you get it?"

"It's the same one you broke," Freckles said, grinning. "My father glued it together again for you."

10

"Strike one!" yelled the umpire.

Martin rested the bat again on his shoulder. He wasn't worried about having a strike called on him. This was his fourth trip to the plate. Besides hitting a long fly ball that the center fielder had caught in the third inning, he had two hits. One was a single, the other a triple.

Mr. Ginty has sure paid me back for saving his little boy on the street that day, Martin thought. Imagine fixing up the bat so it's like new again! He sure is a wonderful man!

The pitch. "Ball!" boomed the umpire. "One and one!"

The score was 7 to 5. The Tigers were ahead. There was a man on first. It would not hurt to knock in another run. The team that won this game won the trip to the World Series.

"Come on, Marty!" the gang on the bench shouted. "Come on, kid! Hit that apple!"

Then he heard his dad. "Drive it, Marty!"

The pitch came in. He swung. *Crack!* The ball sailed out between left and center fields! Martin dropped the bat and ran. He touched first, second, third — and didn't stop until he crossed home plate!

A home run!

"Hurray, Marty!" everybody roared.

Rick caught him and shook his hand. "Thataboy, Marty! Thataboy!"

"Nice going, Marty!" exclaimed Coach Cassell. "Guess we'll be heading for the World Series game!"

Martin's heart beat so fast he thought it would leap right out of his shirt.

The Bears lost hope after Martin's long clout. They didn't score any more runs. The Tigers won, 9 to 5.

Jeannie ran to her brother right after the game and hugged him. Then came his father and mother. Then Barry Welton.

"You'll be a big leaguer one of these days, Martin," Barry said.

Martin beamed, then shook his head. "I can't use this bat all my life," he said, holding up the bat. "It'll be too small for me when I grow up!"

Then another voice broke in, a soft voice that Martin had heard only once before. "Martin, I have a confession to make. I hope you'll forgive me if I tell you."

Martin looked around. It was Mr. Ginty,

56

Freckles's father. Martin was puzzled. "What do you mean, Mr. Ginty?" he said.

"I made that bat, Martin."

Martin stared. His heart flew to his throat. "You — you mean it isn't the one I used to have? The one that Barry gave me? The one I busted in two?"

"No, it isn't. I don't think I could ever fix that other one up so that you could use it again. This is a brand-new bat. I made it myself — just for you."

Martin swallowed hard. He put out his hand. Mr. Ginty shook it. "Thanks, Mr. Ginty!" Martin said. "Thanks a lot!"

Then he turned to his dad. He could barely see him through the tears that blurred his eyes. His father smiled back.

"You see? It wasn't the bat, was it, son?" he said.

Martin shook his head.

It was just him.